A Writer Like You

Sasenarine Persaud

We acknowledge the support of the Canada Council for the Arts for our publishing program. We also acknowledge support from the Ontario Arts Council.

National Library of Canada Cataloguing in Publication

Persaud, Sasenarine, 1958-
   A writer like you / Sasenarine Persaud.

Poems.
ISBN 1-894770-04-8

   I. Title.

PS8581.E7495W74 2002   C811'.54   C2002-905469-9
PR9199.3.P437W74 2002

Printed in Canada by Coach House Printing

TSAR Publications
P. O. Box 6996, Station A
Toronto, Ontario M5W 1X7
Canada

www.tsarbooks.com

CONTENTS

FATHER AND SON CONTEMPLATING BOXING DAY

Unswirling, straight and softly
softly softly falling. Flurries like dots
from the finest fountain pen nib—the day
after—a word you scratch out not wanting
to whore it, or whore this poem:
the million-dollar endorsements
by the million-dollar men running
the fastest hundred meters ads on tv's
soundsight bites. Falling softer
than a million finepin pricks building
on that other season's storms
unable to paint the page rightly until
now weathered muse permitting. Perhaps
soon go south again, sooner than you think
time's running out—just get one snowfall
rightly once and these snowstorms won't be
wasted. A winter just started, a raga spinning
night loves on the disc and the baby
already up and crawling, balancing uncares
of tomorrow with today's wanting to be
hoisted to the window. Tugging at pants
seam and falling softly on the cushioned
diaper. Yes son? Outside, today of the night
echoing children's laughter from the slopes
below, tonight of the treelimbs below
anointed with this cream of season—wave
child wave and mono-syllable the precipitation
ga, da, ma, ba—this unswirling straight
and softly falling cloudust. And maybe once
if we are lucky it paints our page wrongly
rightly rightly—no Milne slighted for pooh
waiting half a century to articulate
father-son laundry.

FATHERING

The stroller tracks in the gravel trail our
own. The quiet August morning in the park
not: dogs led by the ageing German couple
along the rim of trees. The pickup woman
stopping nearby; alone with her two dogs
disappearing down another trail: pebbles
discoloured by the sap of apples smashed
from the fall in last night's rain, the
metroparks worker jumping out his motorized
buggy, sanitizing the grass with a litter
harpoon. And we must watch the time, check
the temperature of the bottled formula
get you fed, get you home on time for
cereal, the cleanup, the morning nap. And
we are only passing the dogwood tree
already bloomed in the spring, another
time when these walks were all my own—
tracks the stroller cannot negotiate
up the hill. And your inheritance on paper
(can I ever be a good and proper father)
perhaps, lighting spirit of spirit
genes—ego covered in science—of souls.

THE HUNGRIEST HAWK

The hungriest hawk you had seen
circling over and over and around
the woods in the valley bleached
by droppings from a dying December
sky, overcast except for sunstarved
conifers: pines and spruces
an unhealthy lemongreen; the ground
layered like a bed with a freshly
laundered white duvet.

If anything moves:
squirrel, fox, mouse or mole even
spectacled eyes would see—if anything
moves the hawk would have its holiday
feast—and a morsel for the new year
assuming birds count time according to
Georgian calendar. Warm and well fed
you joke: the hawk might be Hindu and
what would it be then? What year? 5104?

Nothing moves on
the snowlit ground, among the radar of
the watched. And this hawk circles and
circles and sways its head sideways
downways and circles painfully slow
out of sight, out over the furthest
reaches of the suburban woods and you
feel sorry sorry sorry sorry sorry
enough to excuse this hungriest hawk
you had ever seen, its dive—you turn
your face away—for the rodent.

DRIVING THE BABY

A spruce tipping the shadows of dawn, a gull
wheeling on its white wingtips eliciting
a twinkle of palms and laughter framed
in the rear-view mirror—the bird we take
for granted or this roseblue morning
clear as the darshan of a rishi, a sky
only winter miracles after days of that
winterscaped dark no one wants to talk about—
acceptance of a northern season: dharma's
time: the antithesis of snowbirds-returned
reluctantly: Miami days warm and youthing
left behind in Alligator Alley; great blue

3

herons gliding into the 'glades around
the backs of full-sized alligators waiting
for a feast we cannot see—motoring along
(on cruise control) for the Clearwater sand
as tender as the powder-white Canadian
flour from the prairies. And we are sitting
in the shallows, munching: you between mammam's
legs waving at the gulls circling over heads
and flinging laughter into the gulf
our snacks looped to the birds, somebody
whipping out a camera—the older couple
nesting palm in palm, sandals hanging down
from hands, strolling into the sunset—
we were young once and then maybe not.

GETTING INTO HISTORY

About the doctor saying, "a routine checkup"
and mommy glowing like a tree-ripened
orange—a colour you would come to possess
and redefine! About how we believed the
doctor—no morning or evening sickness
and laughing, walked through light flurries
to the hospital the next day which became
your day before. Something about pressure
not quite right: rooms with drawn blinds
nurses—other women on nearby beds waiting
black tubes wrapped around arms inflating
laughter clipped in: *spend a few minutes*
think about it—consulting in another room
no choice really. The prepacked bag still
at home. About wondering if you were
wondering what was all this pushing and
heaving—an entire night and nothing save
the epidural for the pain—to talk about
the longest night and the longest day

4

until another doctor decided on the section
suited up in lemongrassgreen: the anesthetic
administered by an expert—another doctor
who walked with reading matter. About that
first cry you uttered, a nurse giving a time
check 3:21—another weight and, *a boy a boy!*
About wondering about mommy still dazed
and being stitched up. Those brown eyes
sharp as the song of a robin at dawn staring
boldly, *you o you so you—I heard your*
voice as the nurse placed you in my arms.
And how we peeped at mommy still dazed. About
how they took you away and how you wailed
in the tiny glass capsule helpless, waiting
for her to come to. About walking away
in the late night flurries. Snowflakes
dancing down the day after, as it dances down
now like your pattering feet, arms that
would stretch through the window glass
for that something we cannot see, but know.

GANDHI OFF BROADWAY

A year after we'd delivered the manuscripts
—you were within amniotic—not creeping
yet and suspended in a haversack by
fisher-price: ones advertised to make
mothers look like they have taken back
their no-nonsense lives—stylishly. Do
fathers rear babies?—emerging from
the N line heading for Macy's. That mall
nearby for lunch from the sixth or seventh
heaven overlooking Broadway: orangejuice
cabs like stamps. In the chill spring
sunshine the dark blob of a stone Gandhi
unrecognizable: protest when they put him up

5

in the square—Gandhi off Broadway? Perhaps
one of the pseudos: an Indira or a Sanjay
or a Rajiv or double Sonia—not if Indians
and Italians are cousins! We know the Roman
Emperor brought back an Indian cook: all those
Indian spices now Italian spices in Italian
cookbooks and recipes, and the Indian bigan
transposed to eggplant—only pizza as Italian
as eggplant parmesan. The Roma, our despised
cousins of Europe, those dark gypsies Hitler
almost exterminated: percentagewise this
the forgotten holocaust—O the Ashkenazi
O yes the Ashkenazim! Giving you a little finger
a trick the Jewish nurse taught us in Toronto
always working until the formula: the histories
of cows we hold sacred encoded in the powder
we have liquefied. Bapu liked goat's milk.
India in turmoil, the Empire cracking bottom
up but the man concentrating on a nipple
on-off Broadway for the journalists—mahatma
in the making: a book, a play to hit the list
that one editor afraid to trust her instincts
relying on readers and Agents. Nothing
unsolicited. Who ever heard of poetry hitting
the list? But that inconsequential up here
on the sixth or seventh, above the postagestamp
cars clogging the streets, scraggly magnolias
in parkettes and rare spaces set to bloom
the ginkgo from China adopting well to
steel and stone, stars and stripes and the
beggars at the corner and the pickpocket
of Mr Sammler's Planet mingling uneasily
with more elegantly dressed hustlers—
power lunches or not: homes we have only
in our heads after negotiating black tunnels
under the city. We will cross the river
—this our Ganga—the old line like waters
of this and all rivers and oceans touching

at some point and travelling back to their
sources like Szymborska's "Love at First Sight"
nothing just happenstance—today the gift
generational consciousness. Looking up down.

RELATIVE PASSING

Write how many books
and still missing something
in the funeral home disguised
as a hotel lecture room.

We can sit at the back
with the older men who always
line the wall and seem full
of spunk: a comment or a greeting to

an old acquaintance during the sermon
the chanting of dhuns, drawing a glare.
Men who refuse to walk near
the open casket, or the elegantly dhotied

pandit—a rarity in these metropolises
of the north. The younger priests trading
dhoti for white trousers—"it is not the dress
but the philosophy!" The pandit answers all

"Finally: Truth is Death." To see these older
men's faces or thoughts—to see our own!
We are invincible, unvanquishedable

NO ELEGY FOR DR J

Cheddi Bharat Jagan 1918—1997

Corentyne Thunder blasting through colonial clouds
from Georgetown street corners—"Nobody had ever heard
anybody speak like that before—I joined up right away."

Returning that first time from America with the coveted Dr
and the soon familiar doc: the white Jewish wife; a handbag
of stories of Gandhi nonviolently dismantling the Raj—
copies of the autobiographies of the Mahatma and Nehru
commingling with Marx and the Great October Revolutionist.

Corentyne Thunder raging in Demerara, rousting Martin Carter
to his later genius poems, "This Is the Dark Time, My Love,"
"Black Friday," and "University of Hunger": Wilson Harris and
Jan Carew all writing for the party organ *Thunder*. Twenty-nine
and the youngest elected member of the of the BG legislature.
Doc doc doc singing Cheddi Cheddi Cheddi at your victory in '53

Churchill, aging and smelling of senility, sailing British
gunboats for Demerara: the red-faced British boys empowered
in Indian Khaki drill uniforms and leather boots being told
the red jhandi-puja flags of Hindus were symbols of Communists
International. And Castro had not yet gone to the mountains
much less come down—Che yet comfortable in the South American
middle class. But which propaganda followed you to the country

sides—the peasants unconcerned about your Marx and Lenin
and your pronouncements on the Imperialists. You were Indian
and they were Indian. You were the son of a plantation and
the bitter-sweet sugar, they the cutlasses between canerows
and punt trenches, the ants who fed the mills. They the Booka
serfs. You the Corentyne Thunder breaking through the Booka
clouds and demanding better pay and better working conditions.

You daring to raise your thunder and your finger, your
rishi-wrath against the white god Booka. Tremors—

8

Washington and Westminster putting heads together
Concocting ways. *Who this little coolie? Who that greedy
shark-suited blackman? Let us play them against each other
split them down the ranks.* And they would jail you still
in pajamas, rip up your home; as if a disciple of Gandhi
could ever hide guns or explosives: a disciple of Gandhi
could only hide his prayers and his pujas, the Bhagavadagita's
Krishna exhorting Arjuna—rouse yourself from this stupor
and stand to your dharma as a kshatriya, therefore fight.

You hadn't lost that thunder—only, we thought, the thunder
of the thunder: those philosophies of Gandhi's ancestors
and mine and yours you would turn aside from—the pujas
you couldn't make time to attend, the kathas, the ancient
stories and rites. But they followed you still, in office
and out. You were Indian and that enough for our mothers

growing bigger in wombs and, postpartum, leading marches
and demonstrations, waving banners, answering your calls.

Your white wife who could wear a sari, who didn't scorn the
hovels of in-laws and relatives and the Booka-poor: your wife
who stood up with fire in her eyes to accompany your thunder

that heady time your people returned you to office after
the suspended constitution: first premier of BG—first
local boy to inhabit the Red House in Kingston. That old
capital of the British and the Dutch. And if not enough
again in '61 when they laughed at "TheJaganNightSchool"
your vision of what would become the University of Guyana
or how they would fight for Chairs a long time after that
President, frustrated with his Monroesque affairs, let fly
dogs of destabilization with the racists out of office
waiting to burn Georgetown to the ground, waiting to loot Indian
stores in daylight. And the laughing black policemen watching
the rapes at Wismar, the rapes at Wismar, the rapes. . .

But we shouldn't say such things of the past even with the

9

racists out of power. We knew you then. Critical Support for
the dictator nationalizing King Sugar and Lord Bauxite, and
the foreign banks. We turned our faces away until that sugar
strike when the black soldiers were forced into the fields
as scabs, and the Indians came to you: to the man who said No
to the violence (an Indian army in training in the Creek); you
the man who said No to the Indian farmers who said, *Doc dhis*
a rrasspass. Dhem blackman dhis only respect abhi if we teach
dhem rrass wan lesson. Leh we starve dhem ass out. Leh we tek
out we gun from dhe ground and dhem plastic wrappers. Leh we
farm we own country, stap dhis blackman rrasspass!

No you said. No and No and No when a lesser would have said yes.

Thinking you had lost your balls and your thunder: and when the
young
and disillusioned left in ones and twos and dozens and hundreds and

thousands for the cold you remained nursing that hammer. . .that
day we
invited you to our class on the socialist upheavals of Europe. And
the authorities, scared, wouldn't give you a private classroom for
your lecture: a corner of the auditorium of that building in which
you had started "TheJaganNightSchool" become University, where
young boys blasted badminton shuttlecocks around and you as calm
as a great and graying, balding ancient rishi while we waited
for that thunder witnessed the previous year when they rigged the
elections, threw the Indian polling agents out of the trucks with
the ballot boxes, gunbutted their faces. That campaign of '72

the tractor throbbing in the distance to power the generator. Indians
coming from every end of the Polder: young, old, man, woman, child
barefooted and slippered, on bicycle, on ford and massey-ferguson
tractortrailers: with bottlelamps, juglamps, kerosenelamps, gaslamps
and then after the count they said our thousands gave you just 29
votes
and sent in the army—not redfaced British boys from the blackwatch
regiment—blackfacedboys this time from the Guyana Defence Force

enforcing the curfew. Nobody moves after dark and nothing walks at night save the dark jumbies in leather boots and triggerready fingers.

So you came in daylight. And the army followed gunready in jeeps—old American issue—and we were scared. Would one frightened boy in American fatigues press a trigger, hurl a teargas canister? Even those boys must have been relieved when you whipped out your thunder,
relieved to hear that boom of ages: your truth its own balm and ours.

Not that you cared if they had shot you down in the South American sunshine. What the papers couldn't print you voiced across the black water canal and the dam: a thunder we would always take with us here in the false summers and blustery winters: that time in the Toronto restaurant on the eve of the '92 elections when they asked me to read a poem in your honour, and you came up before and asked
"What about that biography you were writing about me since way when?"

Canada had caught up with me. You moved on. That time in your office
in '88 unforgetting your tart white secretary always appraising you of the intent, always arranging meetings for us and forgetting until I turned up and bumped into you on your break and blurting out in frustration, and you sat me down like a son and worked out my steam:
I could come anytime for the interviews and what if I were not a member
of your party or even a socialist—who better to do your biography?

It was the greatest vote of confidence in my writing I would ever get and we knew I couldn't look back—not then, not now. One hundred things intervening in what seemed like an hundred years and
when everybody ceased believing—even I said you were a fool, words
couldn't do it and for sure words didn't do it—you came back after

11

the twentyeightyear doldrums and won that election. Your excellency
Jagan, the old doc back, the biographyhunters scenting megacontracts
and bookdeals falling at your feet like snow from a winterstorm sky.

I save my one question. The one it seemed you answered early but
no one saw. All I wanted was five minutes of your Canadian State
Visit. But I was not an insider and I never promised a favourable
piece—I could only promise a truth as I saw it—as you always
taught us to see it. Tell the doc it is me, I told them. And you
agreed. After the speech at York University on The New World
Economic Order, after the picture taking and the laughter, after
the drinks and the wholesome "food from home" someone found us
a corner. And you didn't forget that biography I could never start
or finish: my one question prefaced with the reference to all
the criticisms of the pujas you never gave or attended—

"Do you consider yourself Indian, Hindu?"

Reading they would cremate you today I found that recording.

Your old thunder rising above the cackle and clink of glasses and
laughter, "I am not a religious man. I don't have time for that
kind of thing—let them who are religious do that but—" the long
fecund pause one waits a lifetime for, that something you were dying

to say, that something which could jumpstart my book, whatever
book
now unimportant, that something of your greatest something for us,
"But I've never joined any other faith, or religion or following."

Yes—no, not even Marx or Lenin or Nehru or Gandhi.

"A non-practising Hindu?"

"Yes—that's right!"

12

Words with which to place with you on the pyre on the seashore
of a thousand miles. A Hindu on the burning logs on the Corentyne
Coast—Corentyne Bhai finally come home, we hear your Corentyne
Thunder as the flames cackle amidst the dhuns and bhajans—
as a clump of snow quivers and falls in the sunshine on this
whitedrenched morning cluster of pinetrees, green as the courida
and mangrove somewhere nearby, the flames the television cameras
will replay, that heat I know in this unending March snowshine

O Corentyne Thunder, O Corentyne Bhai come home come home
to the Wild Coast of South America—ashes to be strewn in the
Atlantic with jasmine, madar and oleander; ashes of the Corentyne
Thunder we will take with us to the corners of the earth—even
touching the waters of the sacred confluence of Ganga and Yamuna
—pilgrimages, mental or non-mental, energizing us forever.

DO NOT BE SO BITTER

Do not be so like neem or
Karilla, brother who stayed behind
who braved an hundred lines I've erased
from paper, computer documents, mind
potholes unremembered, thieves
lording nights of fitful sleep, days
weighted with: where the lunch of today
or tomorrow's dinner, the few dollars more
to make rates and taxes, the pink electric
bills, all forgotten in this time's slick
repackaging—these tears no one must
see: the little imp of energy—generator
of hope, the focused mind netted
in eyes convinced dreams will concretize
droplets no mother sees: or a son sick and
sobbing in the night—cough, cold, flu and
technology helpless to prevent, or cure
what must run its course. Viruses thriving

13

in this unflappable northern refrigerator
strains arriving with the latest émigrés
from Africa and Asia—each more deadly
than that last flight, laughing the futility
of antibiotics: the once touted medical
miracle—tears no one hears, wailing
for that equatorial heat of Shiva
transforming bacteria, this heat of Shiva

Warmth of friends and family and roots
from which cowards flee and fools justify—
O brother who stayed behind and braved
an hundred things I've erased from mind
do not be so, like neem, bitter at my flight. . .

DISMEMBERING H-INDIA

To sit in the shaded light of a hallucinating
spring night scanning Patanjali's Yoga Sutra
while these two poets argue India: *one sign*
great sage grammarian, one aphorism to clear
this path between mind and mind

> "Aptitude is the process of conducting
> what is tasteful to one and trying to
> establish it. It exists even with the
> learned."

And aptitude is a complication of the mind
with reviews from Los Angeles: the poet-
professor resident in Massachusetts and once
of India (though he might say Kashmir, with
emphasis, ignoring Kashmir of alien Arabia)
professorpoet intoxicated with the Mexican
reason of Paz—that Islam offered Hindus
a chance to free themselves from

14

"(the terrible law of karma)"

That Amherst Agha smug and agreeing
to dislike the philosophies of *Hind*—
or was that Sindh? Who confusing tongues

with throats—Ah, I have no claim to Delhi
or *Mumbai*, much less Kashmir ki Valley
Amherst ki Ali's dear natalplace (from afar)
and I've not visited, like the Mexican Paz, as
attaché as ambassador as bride ki foreign
husband. Just, not merely, ancestral memory
enough: these Canadian monarch butterflies
wintering in Mexico, and knowing about this
die die die die four generations until
the next remembering that summer in eastern
Canada. How to stop the Mexicanborn
monarch butterfly from its summer Ontario home?
You cannot think such things: four into one
hundred and fifty years (and change) of
indenture and emancipation and exile is only
two even using vegetarian mathematics: sixty
years a cycle. This "terrible law of karma"
cannot understand if the seed is of the willow
how expect pears from the willow tree, except

by grafting, not thirties Chicago, Shiva giving
Ganesha the elephant's head. A reincarnation of
repeated trips from Mexico for a sip
of monsoon air:—a gazillion breaths failing
to unravel the essence and being and birthing
of air of air's gravi-capsule theories burning

round a sun of Kashmir ki Ali's logic: such gifts
as art and architecture (17 times sons of Arabia
razed that great temple of *Somnatha*)—I confess
I am already cofused. The Taj a wonder of a diseased
mogul on the backs of 50,000 labourers—mostly

15

Hindus to be sure—imprisoned by an equally
diseased son. To build for the dead and not
for the living Pharaohs enslaved Africa, enslaved
those chosen, those so chosen people—
O let my people go! And yet, Paz, "India owes

not a single new or original thought to Islam."
And this Paz "intoxicates" Amherst ki Kashmir
ki Ali ki professorpoet "with reason" and logic.

If a rotting caste system is Hinduism
is a madman's fatwah or the Amin feeding
human limbs to fishes in Lake Victoria
and eating feared enemies' brains (or so
it is reported) Islam?
Two poets arguing India, one having never heard
of soul or yoga—and that leveling process, an egalitarian
ism, existing before Arabia took to monsoon screaming
on thatched roofs—*conversion is the highest*
form of disrespect, the most debilitating
caste system which says there are no levels of
goodness or function just: I and mine alone
are good and pure; all others unbelievers.

BALGOBIN KHAPPAH

Ehem—is me Khappah—Balgobin Khappah
and nah ask me how dha name come yahsuh.
Anyway is me and dhat lang sunofagun Sam
and Ismith and everybadyelse putting lash
on smooth Demerara likah. We gat abhi own cyaar
and drivah tuh. How dhem a Kanida could seh
Guyana babu a starve! Bai and dhem Georgetown
gyaal—mek eyeball a buss—and dhat 'lantic
sea breeze mek romance, pyar hai. And who seh we
attending Burnham Carifesta? Who care if dhe
man is a wan racist dictatah and lack up Georgie

bai Lamming. Writer nat concern with dhat.
Even dhem Caribbean government nat concern
muchless abhi, and abhi a come from wheretoass it
snowing in April. Leh mih tell yuh: Sam mih buddy
gaan—and Andrew, dhat man who respond to lettah
like tomorrarah a 'estiday, gaan. But nat miih
rrass—life still sweet sweet sweet. Maybe ten
more book—and yuh know a like mih lil poke
—fourr five—mih still gat juice—nah worry
'bout dhem politically correct bylaws. Gimme waan
baattle Bajan rum, waan smoke—Mih nah Sir Watah
Raleigh, nobady throwing water on me. Well don't
ask me how abhi dhis come fuh get dhis name—yuh
know how abhi dhis West Indian staan, always giving
matti falsename, but thankyuh thankyuh manijah
fuh dhis oppatunitee: yours humbly Khappah—
Balgobin Khappah—writing from Kanida.

PLAYING CRICKET
IN THE METHODIST HOSPITAL, BROOKLYN

To cross those boundaries
the ball lofted in air—
batblade pulling from off
to on. To run up to stumps
certain of a wicket's fall—
ball beat bat, and players shouting
appeals to heaven. How many
prayers and the umpire still
unmoved. Eyes moving about
softly like swallows in that
South American sky we knew.

This nurse like a childhood
angel taking your closetolife
less hand: *Mr S your friend's*

come all the way from Toronto.
Talk to him—and you too talk
to him, it helps. Yes, remember
that blue sky of a cricketperfect
day: a few cumulus clouds drifting
hazily across vision—such a
morning as today's in Brooklyn's
spring's garden after the ride
on the rusting BQE—The what?

The Brooklyn-Queens Expressway
you laughed that first time
you gave us directions to your
house. Last year, the year
before or...Twenty years ago
that first time—you and I alone
at the crease, in that silence
talking with eyes. You at the
other end willing me to bat on
hold on, to give you, the better
striker, a chance to go after
the runs—and this reversal
is all I can do for you today

friend colleague skipper: *if you*
could cross this boundary, ball
lofted—eyes following it
and something else behind
in that deep distance. *He's not*
really seeing, she returned and
took your hand again, cleared the
throat, left. To will you on for
the sixmonth baby, the other kids
for wifecompanionlove, unfulfilled
potential, mother brother sister.

Even such things as the house
and car, the unenjoyed promotion

the move to Long Island...nothing
required but that consciousness
which traversed the biganbreakfast
time biganlunch time bigandinner
time dictatortime NS. And you did

graduating. And again, and again
in a new land—Columbia or NYU—
a peculiar consciousness, mindset
to come back, to come back
dear friend, come back from beyond.

I say goodbye. *What?* I almost hear
you say this time. I sit in the lobby
and cry—it cleanses heart and soul
and eyes. White flowers bloom—
magnolias from the deep south. For
those of us who keep memory, nothing
is lost, nothing gone, nothing deleted.

DHARMAKEEPERS

I.
Where these twice shipwrecked Indians hang red
jhandi flags on bamboo poles in their front yards:
Richmond Hill-Queens-New York City—badges of
courage and affirmation: India having deserted us
and yet India, we haven't deserted you—entirely.
You having turned aslant making our backs
stronger with yours behind us, bearing standards
these Christian missionaries reluctantly learning
these jhandas are no calls for help, no residues of
a communist conspiracy slowly octopussying the
apple's blare of horns at driverleadfoot, the
roadwise cautious a word left behind in the lust
of snowwhite's bite. And yet in this spring this

city cleaned itself: 103 Ave freshly reasphalted
and marked with yellow and white phosphorous; the
trees on Lefferts Ave laden with blossoms, young
green leaves of oak and maple and European linden
the chestnut blooms like white nuts reaching
for that leafless city, now home, left behind.

Toronto-the-Good experiencing its coldest May
in eighty years, the cherries afraid to flower
the dogwoods thinking of another American
Memorial Day weekend in New England. And these
doggers in the Morningside Park routinely
ignoring the city sign bylaw, *All pets on leashes*
—to scramble the infant out of the way of what
might be a white wolf following a white rollerblader
mistress back to where a lawyer would have already
answered the phone, given a ballpark figure

and who ready to settle out of court—money
as effective as all the enforcement officers—
the NYPD blues appearing in a flash—two more
cars flashing under the train on Liberty Avenue
Officers listening to the screaming woman—
the apprehended man behaving like a certain
kind of spouse—and threatened with a box (or
New York bax), scolded and released into the car;
the package returned to a satisfied woman. NYPDers
now respected Victorians but it works: crime's
down and Giuliani's heading for another term—but
not if the bleeding heart liberals have their way
appealing to jews and chicanos and blacks and, in
another line, deviants—artists and poets and me

II.
Today it is the F train, changing at Lexington—is that
somewhere in the old Britain Sam had left behind when
Moses migrated? It is simple, hold on to the map
on the wall in the No 6 train as though for balance.

Uptown and downtown make sense until this
buxom wench: longnosed, dark eyed, longhaired, long
legged might be Jewish, if you take the stereotype
seriously, turns her computerprintoutpoem to the light
of our Hunter College stop—another name from another
land—the cowboy didn't invent the world, though
the cousin's daughter at last night's dinner, born
and bred in Queens, is convinced: stars and stripes
forever! O where O where does one find a queen? Not
the fairy queens of queer? And where is a Hawaiian
"crowned" Miss World but on Miami Beach? And is York
still newer than its namesake in old England
after all this graffiti and old brownstones and grime
and old overpasses and underpasses? Laughter.
I, another of her mother's funny oldcountry relatives.
But in one of these old buildings on the east side is
the Sloan-Kettering Cancer Research Centre (or Center)
the Science of medicine or language on the cutting edge
of legs waited impatiently all winter for this warm spring
day overlooking the window of a vegetarian lunch
in the SouthEast Asian Restaurant. Or the SouthEast Asian
Exhibit at the Met. A sudden flash the younger Naipaul
making no bones about his non-meatness: and the women
liberated in their support for their male comrades going at it
from behind, outraged at Naipaul's Jane's Jimmy, taking her
brutally from behind in the bush of a small hot
Island. Was it Trinidad? Yes, then we are agreed he is a Hindu
(whore)—the things we do and did and have to do for dharma
not bumming around for money or experience or love. And so
we expose the pujaris who call themselves pandits, occasional
scribblers, hobbyists who call themselves poets, attempting
to keep time and taal—running to the other appointment
and not keeping the aging white woman waiting. Plantation.
Tonight we can talk again, dissect, build, analyze, demolish...

III.
The defiant younger woman on the wall is a lifesized
portrait of a person I knew, or thought I knew. Traces

21

on your face, in your new Manhattan apartment from which
we catch a glimpse of the Hudson River from the narrow
wraparound balcony. A tour up the winding staircase
as the tea brews, a glimpse of the large fourposter—
you alone in it, another thing I think I know. Should we
have gone in to feel the carved posters worn smooth
with years of usage? We did—your cat ahead of us
into the study we do not mean to give up: books filling
the customized bookshelves to the high ceiling, the new
computer backing this city which never sleeps. And now
we are down to the straight, stiff chairs. The tea is brewed
the toast warmed in the kitchen lined with rows of pots and
pans from the South Asian kitchens I knew in my childhood
like the ones you saw on your trips through Asia, the one
you didn't mention in your Landlady's in Bangkok. It is

obligatory we talk around that which is best left unspoken.
The hour slipping by with no breaks in the tightly controlled
conversations. Poets are the first and last users of language
after all—not bodies, bodies are for sculptors—the most
verbose and the leanest, taking the modern paring knife
to words. You are anticipating this trip to India, walking
around Manhattan searching for poems to fill The Collected:
New and Selected commissioned by your editor scenting
mortality: casting your dragnet around this city for
the memories, and merging time and time. Let us sip tea
munch hardbread snacks—I'm a subject too. Nurse this
tension of young and notsoyoung: lines we note for later
lines I hadn't seen before: grandmother slipping in.

That portrait on the wall haunting haunting haunting the
palms of dear a friend, the brushes of a lover. *I can take
the cat up if it bothers you. Yes please.* Walking away with
the creature—Suess—meowing. I know something you're
not supposed to know and—stiff trousers and heavy hips
up that narrow winding staircase. Cathair spotting the chair
and aye, the antique harp in the corner with the broken
strings, the deliberately left unstrung strings. Irish. As in a

22

style, or a period creation of ambience or an uncaring, this
presence of an accumulated life which will not go quietly.

That quip about the black student asking why Hemmingway
seemed such a better writer than Baldwin and your answer:
Because Hemmingway was a better educated writer. The storm
that followed. Baiting. Intellectual sparring your high
ball. We let that go. Another Brahmin. Why do you keep
making all those trips to Asia? Education makes the
educated. But it is writing makes the writer. Or the writer
makes the writing, or writing makes the writing. Person
and pens medium. Ah yes, lest we forget you are going
to India. White liberal women's fascination with the lives
of the oppressed, the Eunuchs—men whose cocks were cut
off to prevent them assaulting the harem, those poor men
still around—forget the beggars picking the garbage heaps.
You will land in Delhi at 3:00 a.m. so you will not have
the litter of shitters shake your western sensibility.
Poverty doesn't sell like sex, even mutilated sex. Ah those
Eunuchs of India or some faroff land—what a book! And if
that fails, the caste system, O the caste system! or the
highly sexed gods, their guardians, their lovers—
the thousand-women harem, the walls of Khajurao.

Well yes it is time, our hour up and we must go—you to your
appointment with your friend—the spark we felt that first
time not igniting now. That was a public place and this too
private a space. Food doled out for pussy. The apartment
left behind, the uniformed doorman nodding as if understanding
the assumption of another such doorman in Miami. We are talking
in the rushhour Fifth Avenue crowd, amongst the ginkgos and oaks
but I am already back in Toronto, back in another book emerging
the sign of a subway line I take unexpectedly. What I meant was:
we are public persons afterall, very private public persons.

DR WRITER

He had read all those translations into English
and knew he could do it too—mistaking Zhivago
for Pasternak: the doctor creating genius pieces
become a national treasure. Did he forget
the snowstorms, the obscurity, exile in Siberia
hiding from madmen? Lenin urging, *Kill a couple*
thousand, fear makes a revolution, fear makes
a nation? Did Pasternak practise medicine? Death
by heartattack on a Moscow street; one glimpse,
one glimpse of Laura stirring the stockcar song:
tell Laura I love her, tell Laura I need her, tell Laura
not to cry, my love for her will never die. No such ballad
but Goa my love—my dot on the Western Ghats
just hop on a plane, money no problem. Zhivago
not permitted in the land of the beautiful & bold
& abundant, not to the successful cardiologist
on lecterns of the world: England, Spain, Brazil...

But was there one day of hunger, one day's absence
from the golden sunsets of Govapuri's aristocrats
hallowed by sonnets from the Portuguese; servants
and foods and gods and ceremonies imbibed from
Da Gamma's peninsula? *Ah, my young friend, pain's*
relative: I had a wife I loved, yet saw the respected
surgeon's wife, my wife, dying and no medicine could
cure her. Crushed my spirit. Yet pain soars in poetry.
I wrote a book and published it; and then more poems
on death, poems other MDs loved in medical

journals. I had a wife, a loving wife—two cars,
a house on the hill, a sun room, a rest room, a
solarium with a view of the Verrazano, a view
of the ocean, all those ships entering and leaving
New York Harbour. Such a view, look! from this crest
of Staten Island. A child at school. A sprawling
terraced garden with pines at the top trickling

24

into flowers at our door, flowers we planned with
our gardener, that pond we fashioned, those fish we
imported: these rare paintings hung in the sitting
room—sun streaming into the spring morning
windows, florescent on the terrazzo tiles, on that
hunted brocade rug, the 19th century chair...

But one day I will leave for Manhattan. This is
beautiful and I love it but I live on an island
away from the literati, writing in a vacuum,
living in a capsule of spring blooms—a large
garden with niches locked out from the house on
the hill, the houses below or about, coves where I
compose in the summer and autumn and spring.
But I live on an island, and I must break from this
academic writing, from this lecturing, from this life

of living and dying, from this mending of hearts,
from this hearing of patients' histories, from this
receiving of guilts and blames from beds of wonder
and waiting for replacement organs, from this
clearing of arteries, from this bypassing of
bypasses, from this view from this hill—yes
it can be bitchy in winter with ice on the edges
of the roadway, ice on the sloped asphalt, curb,
those lingering memories. I know I have to pay

for the critiquing, for the place in Manhattan
for that apartment closer to Sinai in the core
of the apple—as we say here—the heart of the
world, really. The lamplight of literati. Now I
have more time for my music, see my setup. I am
secure. What more to accomplish? Yes suffering's
relative. I had a wife and she died. So I live
on an island in a large house on a hill. I see the
Atlantic and the mouth of the Hudson littered
with ships—if you could see it streaked with mist!

25

I've a terraced garden and a pond with fish,
spring blooms surrounded with words in my head.

That nobel of Arrowsmith, those books of Chopra,
you know, the Ayurveda man, Dr Chopra—
Deepak Chopra who now writes novels. The Dr
and his publicists making him a novelist—I
can do well with no woman's distractions, no
little child's clamour for affection, no worry of
money, no worldly concerns but this thirst for
literature—this immortality of verse, this food
for the soul. This longing for perfect poems,
and perfect stories—you know poetry a stepping
stone for novels—that exquisite book. And I know
you're thinking of the eveningdoctorthing, and why
you can't learn surgery in the evenings
and join me in the OR, yet why I practise evening
poetry and dare stand alongside your pure poets
I didn't say don't give up your dayjob, but writing's
a different thing from surgery and I'm in a hurry up.
Yes, tell that to Walcott or Brodsky or Heaney.

POEM POEM

I'm writing this in secret and nobody must know
Poetry's poetry and poetry's secret
I'm writing this in secret and nobody must know
Poetry's poetry and poetry's poet
I'm writing this in secret and nobody must know
Poetry's poetry and poet's poet
I'm writing this in secret and nobody must know
Poetry's poetry and poem's poem

Where the lines are long and the barbs sharp
The wah-wah's hollow, the compliments skimmed
From today you pat my back and tomorrow me you

To find out why I'm writing this in secret
For when I'm done and ungone so you lip
He was a good man and wrote with passion

So I'm writing this in secret and nobody knows
If nobody knows poetry's poetry and poet's poet

FRAGRANCES

No flavours of almonds or ambergris
or seaweeds here. No scent of seasalt
or even banyans by the sea: we were
sitting on washed concrete in the shade
near the pool when the northern scholar
came out dripping, black pudendum hair
curling round the bikini like black
snakes from a cleft in the Scarborough
Bluffs.

            We couldn't swim in that
chlorined water—not that we wanted to—
but others did: averted our eyes under
the floridabungalowroof shading the
concrete; sandals and polished nails,
snippets of sons and daughters, a scent
of souls mingling.

            The essence of fragrant
Indian oils and spices sprinkled far
away into ma's cake mixes: spoons
turning easily in butter and melting
Demerara sugar—that too from India—
passing smoothly from hands to hands
until time—those looks we always got
and wanted lingered with the fragrance
of the oven.

27

But none of that here today
no scent of ambergris or almonds—and you
anticipating again, "that too from India?"

This morning there is a whiff
of the Morningside willow weeping yellow
leaflets on the late spring cutgrass, fresh and
mixed with the unsalted biscuits the infant
crunches and scatters in the wind for
sparrows and starlings—"bir bir bir"—
these cooy cooy sounds infants and birds
and parents and teachers understand—wisps
of longing and belonging and unbelonging.

THE COOLIE POET

Coolie poet determined to do something
at Oxford following that other don Sir
VSN. Coolie poet wearing jacket and tie
and intoning Britishly at the podium:
how awed to be in the same room with
Naipaul! So what if you have met him
Coolie poet, yet writing so irreverently:
the blasted rhythms of the blasted
Carnival Boy—carnival from tropical
islands sells: did Harris take an
hour to coach in a London pub. Peacock
language? Even Solomon sent to Hind for
peacock feathers (libbers having a ball
with this) to decorate his palace for
Sheba. *Man you've got to understand*
this is a contemporary British thing. We
are an irreverent people. We don't give
a fuck, really, about sacred cows. There's
a tradition look at Rushdie. We had not
yet crossed the causeway to Miami Beach but

her nose was red and peeling and she was
defending you: the Coolie poet who cut
cane and carted luggage at airports,
slaved on the waterfronts of the Amitabh
Bachan Hindi movie but delivered from the
podium Britishly. Or laboured poems and
novels and essays in the Euroform for the
Euromistress: language; *dhis yahso thing*
a bruk rass fuh larn. Mih nah know wha
abhi dhis a gu do rass. But dhis a sell
book staan like ass, rass ki story staan
even dhe Hummingbirdman know dhis rass.

Yes Coolie poet, but if there's white
abstraction isn't there brown and yellow
—who has a monopoly on abstraction—
and, Coolie poet, isn't there Coolie
abstraction too? Whatever that means!

FRESHCUT LILACS IN A ROOM

A curled moon besting the overcast but
not this vase of flowers—*you have to*
give these stems long slits to absorb
moisture, and change the water daily—
sealing the pungent fishfriedinstaleoil
scent attempting to sneak in from the
open balcony door. These snores more
rhythmic than that last time years ago
when that man went over Niagara Falls
in a barrel and swore he'd never never
do that again. And this evening's glow
in the conservation area; one child
running away on the grass and plucking
strings, *mama mama mamaa, dada dadaa*
the other silent in the womb listening

to jets, low and large and loud, level
off for the landing at Pearson, a lone
robin hop hopping on the grass, calling
from a crimson-maple limb—a nuthatch
responding—yes, this has been a late
spring. This glow once igniting that
New York trip when the running child
was enwombed, that long hot day cooled
by a sickle breeze coming off the
Atlantic, an afternoon punctuated by
jets levelling off for La Guardia, and
your snores rolling softly as on sand.
We were alone as now; the same contented
glow on face as this evening when we cut
these lilacs you wanted, these blooms
which perfume this room, pervade this
world, this universe, your orbed womb

ANOTHER COOLIE POET

Great dreams. Mih gat vision man, vision.
Leh mih tell yuh what I'm developing—
mih own verses called Harrans—three
lines long, two short with rhyme scheme
of...like Limerick. If dhem white man...

Harran got up sagely and left. We hadn't
heard from each other in years. And after
another handful of years: *An offering*
fuh mih overseas bruddah—with nuff
respec fuh all yuh accomplishments: in-
scribed in his journal—an accomplishment
Another couple of years and passing
through—he too heading for U London
or some British university to finish up
following dons one two and three and... He
was being harassed in Georgetown, poet Nana

wanting to wring his neck for pretending
to be Hindu and Indian. Another Presbyterian
among the sheep: Hinduism or was that Indian
ism selling, the flock busy nibbling the new
grown grass of identity and open affirmation
after the ironBurnhamyears, unaware watchers
on the hill knowing sheep don't have those
long ears or that sheep don't eat sheep. And
another poet, Hrimm Krimm suing him for
defamation (well this not to be published in
my lifetime) or some such thing for something
in a poem in his journal: *Nah ask mih fuh*
what! Mih lawya ah look afta am. Yuh rass
think mih stupid, dhat mih wan lil bai. An
what dhi fuck dhis—yuh don't believe mih.
I eva lie! Mih had to run lika rass. An mih aan
mih way to Landan! An yuh know how dhem
blackman at Guyana immigration hold yuh up
fuh any lil thing, and wan big big bribe!
Jus like in dhat dunks, mango and pineapple
story about coolieman chineman and blackman!

O dhem Harrans? Rass bai leh me get dah
dactarate fus nah! Yuh nah see how all dhem
bai dactarate give dhem wuk a university,
mek dhem own writing get authority. Yuh nah
see how dhem dactarate mek dhem turn writa.
How all dhem critic feel PhD or foreign
university mek dhem sophisticated writa.
Harrans? Leh me get dhe dactarate fus nah!

WAKING UP

Live on a certain floor—say twelfth
and that remains constant winter after winter
after winter. Reach a certain height
at a certain age and that too remains constant
year after year, until the surfacing memories of
stooped old men and women hidden from
the youthed beaches and parks, until
one latespring morning after the trees have
leafed and the men in white come out to play
cricket, and you hear the jubilant shouts.

A boundary or, appeals to umpires. But you cannot
see the north field anymore. And only the pitch
to the south is visible—the trees having grown
unnoticeably during those summers you were looking
elsewhere: retreed conservation areas and restored
ancient sites, cottage country, other cities
and towns and countries. Next year even the batsmen
at the southern pitch will be close to gone
from vision. And you can go down to that distant
field or flick the telly switch to baseball
because it is too much trouble to find cricket.
You take a cold Canadian blue: let the children
beware, let the wife wash the dishes, cook lunch
as you grow adjusted to the sofa—*honey pass
a cold one—and get this, the bases are loaded.*

And you get up another day still longing
for that cricket bat but baseball is easier
just switch the telly, research—write a book
on Cooperstown your Jerusalem—if players get
millions why should you sit on the sofa and make
Molson breweries richer. And your wife growing
jaded from trying to make you pull your weight
away from your middle, or smug you are no longer
attractive to young things—words you don't write

in poetry, language laziness—receding hairlines,
trousers you blame on the dryer for shrinking
around waistlines. Or happy in her children or an
affair at the office and who cares or notices
until this day you wake up late to the jubilant
shouts, appeals to umpires, the cricket field barely
visible. And you are alone and perspiring profusely:
You cannot chop down all the trees in the woods
but it is not too late. You can move around
those trees of a bad dream—or you can leave:
the writer in the airmail envelope leaping across
the water at your throat like a jaguar: *in the first*
place, I have a difficulty with all of you who left,
or thought you could leave! End of discussion, period!

BACKDAM POET

I.
Writing about all those backdam people, about
all those plantation labourers and sardars
sexing—he preferring f-ing—all those women
from the weeding gang, following the examples
of departed white overseers. Writing about all
those pandits peddling dalpuri and roti
and curry for profit or favour and later whoring
themselves—little wonder the critics (all non-
Hindus until that time he appeared unannounced
in my office) were in awe and applauded.

Not quite the shade of bitumen—we had never met
till then—the balding head camouflaged with
the foreign-looking cap: *Man I've just come back*
from Canada—great guys there, did a few lectures
at York University—and dhey having another
conference. You should all go, make the trip...

33

Later they said how, beered up and with the cold
getting to him, he whipped out his penis—he would
say cock—and peed on the carpet, spraying those
present, how he peed on the sofa. His poet host
near chasing him out in the cold, embarrassed before
his Canadian friends: *so this the gifted old country*
boy who needed a break, all the leeway we can give?
It seemed all arranged; picking up the other poets
meeting another at the favoured drinking spot. More
beers I'd long given up. The woman entering the rum
shop prearranged and his pleading and finally the
cajoling: *you're going to come back home right! I'm*
free as a butterfly. She nodded and left. Smiles all
around. More beers and then conspiratorially: *Mih*
like mih lil pussy. O dhe wife in New Yark. A hope
she neva come back. She had already left him. *You*
guys must come up, come up to mih house Sunday for
a real literary get together. Dhis is only brukice
and I gat a sweet lil pussy waiting fuh mih there…

II.
A jewelled morning along that South American
coast, the browning scrubgrass freckled with sheep,
raisined with black goats and cattle; fresh cowpats
scenting the breeze coming off the sea like a certain
agarbati known in childhood. The acquaintance
from his village cautioning; *mih know he. Live two*
streets from we, real jadubance—obeahman he.
People a guh steady fuh jharay. An nah mek mih tell
yuh wha he a-duh to dhem stupid young gyaal.
Why yuh think he wife left he tail?

It was a house on short stilts, a house he was proud
of, and the huge Shiva lingum in the frontyard like
wearing your Indianness on your chest in an Indian
crowd. The visit to the inner shrine: the books
on the sagging shelves above the worktable a feat
in that time's anti-learning. The tour over, as if on cue

his drinking partner and sounding board, another poet
who served together in the quasi military unit of the
Kabaka appearing. He would later admit: *Mih lucky
if mih gettam once a week—she always too tired from
wuk like if mih nah wuk to.*

They paused between the barealls as though cuing my
turn, hoping I would talk about mine while I waited
for them to continue. We knew who would talk then
and who would not except in verse later: coming on
Walcott afterwards:

> "Poets are in one way nature's idiots. They are
> inarticulate. They are capable of speaking only
> in poetry..."

If at all. But we never met again except in journals
and publications in which our work appeared. And later
someone said, his greatest moment came when Naipaul
visited his house. And like that other Coolie poet
he was awed, perhaps thinking of Rama visiting Nishad,
and wondering if he would turn up in Naipaul's Ramayana.

SARI

I.
There were two sets of ceremonies—one Hindu the other
Christian—for that one of her marriages: brownskinned
browneyed poet—dovelook! and the groom from that Eastern
European country no longer existing. Tito (imagining Burton's
screen performance) was still alive and defied in the Non-aligned
Movement by other non-aligned leaders promoting their turn on
that worldstage: silencing (or butchering) their critics at home.

The one we knew, the third richest black man in the world.
Infrastructure loans from the World Bank, and all manner

of benevolent foreign banks creamed off to Swiss accounts.
The little bully from my father's schoolyard becoming the
presidential bully, Commander-in-Chief—uniform included;
lawyering in England, hooked by Churchill's oratory: peasants
and urban-ghetto-blasters loving their very own mastering
the Queen's English. Such conquests! Fresh young women
and attractive ministers' wives—the deader the ministers the
better—or foreign (white) female dentists, cabaret or kathak
dancers murdered on the seashore for refusing a night with
a visiting black Head-of-State. So it was said. Grandeur! He
should have been massa; riding on horseback whip in hand
on the new state plantation Hope: civil servants in "voluntary
weekend service" labouring at weeding and hoeing—pretend
farming... The ghosts of Dutch slave owners laughing Cuffy
the house slave become revolt general—raping those Dutch
women captured in the plantation house instead of attending
to defences—reincarnated. Dutch reinforcements pouring in.

That black man's black deputy named Best Man, his smile
sending a chill over the local guestrow—not lost among
foreign dignitaries and the diplomatic corps guests. Someone
daring to whisper: he had his time with her already!

And why were we there? For tomorrow when the huge pavilion
would be dismantled and the lawn restored; to sing chowtal,
bring a breeze of colour and perfume for her new husband, show
him the rich folksiness of her land—get his juices flowing?...

And later, after she had become their sponsor and published
their collective verses—hers included, of course—promoter
of the arts; mother, sister, guru—somebody adding concubine—
they came to break my aloofness, plunder my silence. What are

you writing? We know you are? In her newer house, another place.
Rolling trees on that extended green strip like a Shaivic trishul
prodding the Waterworks; the huge saman trees, imported like our
ancestors from the east, flowering and spattering the long grass
swaying in the wind with pregnant seedpods: windows framing

36

a deep blue sky wrestling with probings of art and discourses
on the role of the artist. And while she moved away for those
important phonecalls in her study—the chastizement: how I could
have shown more respect for her, played the game—this woman was
distinguished promoter of India's culture, heroine of her arts…
Didn't I know? Didn't I know the husky voice that seduced
listeners on the air—expounding on the raags, broadcasting them
and Indian High Culture, in a time when only supporters
of the regime got on the air—there being no television then—
and she got on more than most. That time several years before

When I first saw her standing in the afternoon sun like a
Maharani in brocaded sari, waiting for the serfs to come
and extract her British Bean-car from the mud. We on an outing
from the city too, playing billiards in a country rumshop.
Those other friends laughing when I started forward to help;
Whore! How yuh think she get all dhem radioprogramme and dhem
facilities? She fuck all dhem ministers. Roop's voice carrying

to her in the afternoon sun, standing on the muddam arms
folded like a princess in her blue sari waiting for help—
and all these years later Roop's exwife strolling through
the Queens' Center in New York with her new husband: *Man*
whore! He want all dhem lil lil girls in Calgary. Lef he deh. A lef he
rass with dhe mortgage and he lil sportscar and dhe snow…

II.
They say she passes through these northern cities, occasionally
plugging her collection of rifled Indian artifacts to museums;
(she had said: Why don't you bring some of your material. I'd
love to see what you're doing. We've heard a lot about you.
And we can get them published in our next anthology!) visiting
displays—not only museums thrive on the plundered—giving
readings and presenting papers. The trademark sari clinging her
body as gracefully as ever, the husky voice; the cultivated
privacy—if a poet is private—more ordered: whatever happened
to that husband? Who could dare ask of the new tutelaged writers?
And of those who came for me, who praised you to the Indian skies?

37

OTHER SUMMERS

Except for these moments growing larger
those summers drift closer to bedrock with
this bubbling closer to surface—infants'
laughter. We are trying to stay this sunset
which magics age and innocence—an ancient
palm leaning across that not-so-ancient
lighthouse, waves running along stonebreakers
before the seawall like a staccato of tracer
exploding. A delicious scent of shrimp tossed
ashore at high tide drying to shell and who
turned up nose would walk away, and yet would
still hug knees and linger, staring out to sea
at houses on stilts like crimson flamingos at
ocean's edge? To go that far to realize
perspective! What was there in common, what
shared? That we were different painters?
A memory the sex was good, the best
at first—and last? The children sleeping
now the litlamp dimmed—roll a movie, scan
a book, talk. It was not so good as it was
before the cracked up heels, the ageing poet's
misspent middle years where all is assessed
by quantity read-unread. You don't know of the
abuse of underachieving daughters and never
never never never tell this to anyone, my friend.

And we never will. But we've made our peace
dispatched our once bright flags to dusty corners
maintained our long unbroken love of silence.

LAKESIDE

Sitting on the smooth waterwashed pebbles
and plopping the clear water alternately—
the children demonstrating to the clumps
of sitters on the grassed hill, in the shade
of pines and aspens, we might have been
undoing doers, were it not for you.

Poetry gone out across the lake, downriver
to the ocean, writing taking a hike—no
new phrases, no new way of saying the same
old things for love and death and birth
and inertia and all the classic vices of writing.

Here on the water's edge only children
are wading with parents standing guard
focused on any act which might become
mishap on the smooth pebbles, in the clear
cool water, in an afternoon sun where
boats hoist sails to catch the light wind.

like that couple on the hill, and their children
teasing the kite. And why do you, noticing
the kite, suddenly change step, and dash
downhill, and for the roll of string slipping out
the flyer's fist unto the clipped green grass?

BIRDS

This coo coo coo cooing pigeons make
this humid July morning, was that first
sound we heard from the infant, sleeping
through the grass cutter and the sparrows'
songs penetrating the helpless sentry
of an open balcony door. Someone bangs

a lid shut on shouts of children playing
in the parking lot. School closed
for the summer, we sling-shoted birds—
those slowly pigeons prime targets
despite the scoldings accompanied by the
later unspoken: *pigeons nesting on a roof*
a sure sign of wealth. A bird, Garuda, was
Vishnu's divine transponder. Even Darwin
used birds in his evolution theory. Pigeons
or rockdoves, more Audubon-Society-Field-
Guide-to-North-American-Birds correctly,
flapping and fracturing the thick still
morning air. The baby coming late in fall
—snow already on the ground, the windows
just sealed, the doors closed against
the cold—how could he have heard such
sounds? Were we too worried with the wailing
to notice them crowding the windbreaking
ledges, or to recall the summer in the womb,
the summer in the learning womb, the summer
in...? All these questions kids ask for us
and then swiftly turn to other playthings
as if it is all of no consequence—
Are we who, or what intuition, we imitate?

UNDER THE MULBERRY TREE
IN THE MORNINGSIDE PARK

Home home home sings this laden tree:
notes from previous places and lives
bursting a Varanasi-sari-red on fingers
and faces; these ripe fruits which robins
ravish unabashedly in the dense foliage
and on the tantalizingly peppered grass.

Unable to resist the aroma of early summer
sloped on decreasing daylight, too minute
to notice now. This cool spell might be
spring with a few lilacs still in flower,
the weeping willow still a lemongreen
graceful young. Three days after that
Island's return to a China slowly losing
its redness —we notice the coincidence—
two women, and a man, we assume
HongKongChinese resettled, sunning
on the parkinglot tarmac and racing their
dwarfdog, and staring at us unabashedly;
intruders in the mulberry's shade.

What tree that? What wild fruit
you and bird find so tasty?
You sure it safe? No thank you?

Cut off too long from that ancient mainland
or too schooled in the financial markets
to remember this tree which ancient China
gave to silkworms which gave finest silks
to Marco Polo not wanting to return home.

Vickramaditya, the ancient Hindu
king, journeying to the Emperor's capital
for his bride: that Chinese princess who
knew the secrets of silk, who restored his
limbs in the lamplight of raag Dipaka, who
gave him love and journeyed back to Ujjain
with him, taking this mulberry tree under
which we feast on the ripe fruit, and dream
of rich Varanasi silk saris—of stillfresh love.

41

SUMACS

Let me tell you this now we speak only through
short sentences: these small trees you asked
about in the fall, envious of their velvetred
fruitclusters are blooming on this July fourth
morning when we might have been proceeding
for The Big Bash on the hyperbole day. Or
watching World Cup football-soccer anxious:
would America be eliminated? That answer we knew
though for an hour the sky...and then laughter.
Somebody made a big splash in the pool, beers
flowed and bodies rocked to what might have been
reggae or calypso. And from our corner literature
like molten lava rolling through a Montserrat
mountain gap and genderpolitics. Mircea and
Maitreyi. That Mircea Eliade-Romanian-novelist-
seeker-Indophile-philosopher-romancing-with-his-
guru's-sixteen-year-old-Bengali-daughter-and-in-
fiction-rupturing-her-virginity? That Maitreyi
Devi-for-American-feminist-up-in-arms-with-her-
claim-the-rupturing-was-not-then-not-him-not-
never-response-novel-forty-years-later. Would we
end up the same? Coming to the American south,
wronging the Southern Woman—so many examples
even Scott—in fiction, and who to write
a response and who famous, whose child...the
literary friends only suspecting the seductions
and your camp cautioning: *be careful what you,
who you write! South Florida's a seductive place
its heat addictive and mindaltering.* Like this
northern summer and these northern trees asked
and unnamed in that effusive silence blooming
coneshaped corncoloured clusters waiting for
another redsilver fall.

MIH CALL DHIS WAN "COOLIE WRITAH"

"coolie man coolie mai wuk man bruk man wuk
mai baan fuh wuk baan fuh mek wuk stap wuk
done wuk eat wuk suck wuk—coolie man coolie
mai coolie scribe bruk he backside fallawing
whiteman language bite out whiteman pencil
fuh mek dhis coolie mai coolie man poetry I
man a wan coolie man poetbrother of all dhem
blackbrothers struggle in Angola and South
Africa and yes right hey in Kanida and nah
fuget mih wan honourary feminist—hope dhe
feminist press publish mih blasted poetry
book—look advantage dhem man a tek pun dhem
woman dhis—abhi own sista but dhis man
coolie man get converted by dhem kanadian
Presbyterian churchman jus fuh get wan
education—wan miseducation yuh think mih
stupid dhem think mih stupid I man coolie
man ain't baan fuh wuk but all dhem coolie
man coolie mai coolie bai a Guyana who mek
wuk wan fuh bruk wuk—well abhi a ketch dhem
rass when abhi a guh to Guyana in august fuh
crusade—mih still with dhe Presbyterian
church yuk know and all dhem coolie mai
coolie man coolie bai who mek wuk done wuk
bruk wuk leh dhem rass come hey leh dhem
rass come hey through Christ our lord and
sevya leh dhem rass come to Kanida and leh
mih mek wan nada commission—wha yuh think a
mih day jab—but mih still baan fuh be
wan coolie writah—wan coolie crabdag writah
well thank yuh thank yuh mih bruddas an sistas"

WEST INDIAN IN SNOW

Laughing at this coarseness of language
in the performance: that something poets
are supposed to define on the page
an obsession with intellect which revels
in that usage—the white streets left
behind, the frigid February air melting
inside a blackness everywhere. Long faces
waiting for a touch of tropics: the talk
of cricket, seagrapes instead of raisins
mangoes instead of apples; a kind
of ostrich burying its head
in the sand—well make that a crabdog
burying its head in snow. The tables
lined with Demerara rums and the coolie
poet taking the microphone. We learnt
a long time back how to pander to
the crowd and mass market—the
customer is always right, the consumer
comes first—drinking the distilled
urine of cane: that plantation empire
thing like a rapist's penis we learn
to take flight from, the microphone:

coolieman beat blackman backside
blackman beat coolieman backside, licks
like ass—is dhe raceriots sixties and
blackman beat coolieman rass coolieman
beat blackman ass but yahsuh a Kanida
abhi a all waan, yes abhi all waan West
Indian nation but dhem is stupid stupid
people mih tell yuh—what dhe chorus?
Coolieman pelt lash a blackman rass and
blackman pelt lash a coolieman rass—
fugetting Gandhi and Martin Luther (na mind
he come afta)—an' thank yuh thank yuh all.

44

Humour the best medicine
for scars which will not go away
from society which trivializes
its ugliest acts, performs them for two
dime laughter: flaky poems of affirmation:
see mih nah loose mih kultyah. But Sunday
morning tie and jacket and the Canadian
Presbyterian church. We leave warmer and
hungrier, playtimefull with this—
poverty of poetry or poetry of poverty?

PETROGLYPHS

Closer, the blackeyed Susan is not so black at all,
golden petals spinning July sunshine to the butterfly—
that very monarch you would chase into the uncut grass
along the water's edge: nothing Scottish about the scotch
thistle the curious childhood fingers grasp gingerly.
Some things we smell, some thing we touch: wild marigolds
along the trails of the ancients, this sacred rock
an altar and a tabletop with the drawings of shamans,
those Algonquian medicinemen—persons—now neuterized.
Nanabush in rabbit form—remember bunny—son of
an Algonquian and a spirit person. And these tourists
who read and nod sagely; outside, laugh at Pavan Putra:
Hanuman, son of Anjanie and the windgod, because India
has no sense of history, crams her offsprings' heads
with myths as colourful as the jacket of the
FolktalesfromIndia book edited by Ramanujan. Rocks
bare: these etchings on the Canadian shield dark
to fading from weathering. We have put up a glass-sided
building to hold for posterity, for the curious other
Indian poets from another end of the world to compose
nickel lines, feel moved. And only your little feet racing
the edges, face neatly through the bars staring as adults
do. This is a sacred place—we assume. But your

feet patter the silence, fingers pointing the ceiling
fans, a celebration running round and round, a freedom
we had lost and found again. The ponytailed warden
understanding your joy—there's a nature booklet
for kids, wooden blocks, paper and crayons for replicas
of Nanabush or...who could take any shape—like Hanuman—
and yet get trapped in the actions of that shape assumed—
baby mother father warden—stepping into sunshine, the
pebbly trail cheered by the crowd of wild marigolds, the
whitebanded black butterfly dancing through the heat and
humidity and the bright sunlight, the crunch of biscuits
on the shaded trail: oaks and pines. A time when people
dreamt and dared to etch dreams on—what seemed
like eternal—stone. Fingers letting go the crumbs
and unchewed fragments in a sound celluloid sleep.

ENDING JULY

This midsummer creek rages beyond those bushes
and wildgroundcover showered with wildflowers
we have yet to locate and name in those
volumes on shelves. "How to make a garden."
Even with wildflowers no longer wild...

And waves roaring over rocks: if we didn't
know the ocean's location, this disorienting
sound might be last night's thunderstorms.
A deluge and this morning that girl
who loved to watch frogs—so they reported—
was sucked in over another lifeline.
Forty-five minutes later creek already
stalking lungs and stonedead.

What water didn't do, rocks did.
Midsummer still? For seers who are scribes
who can see the future and record: this

is the halfway point of this life! And we
have yet to near that high mark when water
burst and baby comes. Another cry of paradox?
To be parents and unglad.

And all these flowers which line the roaring
stream and fan air, decorate grass and under
brush as in the weave of your petticoat:
like things we put off for another life
not here not there. That summer we ended
and didn't. Midsummer which isn't.

FULL MOON

Waking ripe in morning night
the luminous clock tickling
the sky: if you look towards
the lighted city you cannot
find stars. You must head
for the Kawarthas. For cottage
country's summer obsession
of yuppies—Goldie Hawn & Kurt
Russell from NewYorkHollywood
not excluded. Yes, our cottage
this, our cottage that and you
Canadians allowing no privacy
well yes it's really a mansion
in cottage country and we are stars but...
We would be content
to own our apartment and yet
as renters do—until rent act
repeal—we do: this balcony
our lab for facing sky and
hot summer nights: if eyes grow
accustomed to dark eyes grow
accustomed to light everywhere
And stars must outmoon moon.

47

FLIGHT ARRIVING

An eternity to descend—even the infant
is bored—too long a swing around the city
over the old Bruce Mill—a place where
a Bruce of Scotland finally came to rest
anew with abundant lands and fertile soils
a long way across the cold ocean, a long way
from the long knives of ancient hatreds
from highlands and lowlands and if there are
heathens, the Kirk of Scotland. Who cares?
History is irrelevant except to tourists.
Even the infant is bored. We'd rather see
touchdown. The swift arrival of ancient
feuds. A bomb on Air India taking a drink
near Ireland. Did Joyce have an Ulysses?
Pan Am over Lockerbie and last year's
Olympics receding: the downed TWA flight
over Moriches Beach so close New York
shivers. And hopes the world shivers too.

It was a cold summer even if you didn't
have ac all day. Discords sown coming home
in these vessels' continuous arrivals.
The dispatches of Intelligence agencies
and grieving families still unanswered.
Who or what arrives in the womb of the bird
waiting for a suitable host? Another theory
of reincarnation. When the baby comes. When
the baby comes: this one's wails last fall
the fevered trips to doctors which made you
sit up all night wondering where's the end:
more virulent strains of viruses arriving
from where, from when, thriving in the cold.
And having your attention now—the plane
lower than treetops, the bee darting
among wildflowers and laden grass stalks
must be chased, observed—not that

you are bored but something else grabs
your attention, this here... And what is
behind is behind suddenly. Irreversibly
we have slipped from land to land.
And wherever we walk now is home.

YATRA

(At the End of the Annual Hare Krishna Parade, Toronto)

And we could only spread our blanket on the sand
at the water's edge, in the shade of a marshwillow's
sharp, corrugated trunk which discouraged backresting:
so many miles away so many years and trips along that strip
of Atlantic Coastline from Bel Air to old Fort Groyne
chasing songbirds we have now located in birdbooks.

Birds opting for the Pacific or Central or Mississippi
or Atlantic flyways—these very birds we thought we lost forever
appearing overhead and tweeting—all those springs and falls echoes
from "salt trees" (the chewed leaves salty) like this one
this tree we selected automatically from along this line of lakeshore
curving into New York with a wisp of that trip on the Essequibo
river—the treed islands and the other almostinvisible bank like
canines
scratching at the ocean. Today we do not need binoculars
for those other shorelines, or the group of tandoori teens
plunked down on the sand at the water's edge daring
that one girl in the cheap, purplewhite sari sharing cigarettes now
the crowd is left behind, around tents in the park for the concerts.

Having performed their dharma in the Younge Street Parade to
please
parents obsessed with Krishna Krishna, or some primal need

to frolic and dance, themselves obsessed with that chant of dholak
and jhaal —immersion in a peoplestream bubbling like lava down
Soufiere's top
to the harbour islands' boats for the endofparade picnic.

We could only watch Krishna raked through Canada geese
droppings
and preened duck feathers: red lettering on saffron signs marking
displays—
those same ones we saw last year, grown a little older, a little more
jaded, spiced up with the shaven head of the European monk
holding forth: Hari Bol—greetings in the name of Kreeshna
and our great departed sage Prabhupadha—a soul now writhing
like a wounded cobra. The Toronto chapter of Krishnas
split again. West Virginia split for the golden temple's golden eggs
for every gander owner—white males with bald heads and chandan
streaked forehead, dhotied and mala-ed: their wives behind or
mixing
in brightly coloured saris—tots in tow. Remember Krishna who
frolicked
with gopis, who never condemned copulation or procreation: Hari
Bol!
And our great beloved Prabhupadha brought the mahamantra: Krishna
Krishna
Hare Hare, Rama Rama Hare Hare and also great Jagan-nauth to the west.
He said

We wanted to jump up on a tabletop and shout no no—a lie, another
lie!
To be rubbed so shamelessly again into that opaque sheet of history.
A moving on of European colonialism from India to the Indies. Those
coolies sent to work the sugar plantations not merely coolies. Coming
also
with Rama and Ramayana. Krishna and Gita and Upanishad and
Bhagavatam and Puranas: Rama Lila and Krishna Lila—Mahabharata
and Maha Yatra one hundred years before Prabhupadha. Another
Who didn't read
our history or else who forgot my ancestors who left the Gangetic

50

Plains
from Calcutta, bound for British Guiana, who brought that
mahamanta
west west west...? And yes enjoy the show folks —Hari Bol—Jai Jai
Hari Bol.
No murmur from a crowd waiting for the start of the concert, now
the free vegetarian meal was over: not that we didn't have our lunch
bags and baskets. This year there's a new thing—back to back on the
shared

stage we get two shows for one. From the fringes we catch only
glimpses
of the great classical dances of India, and hear on the other side:
Lovefest.
Krishna bam Hari bam Krishna bam guitar bam, drum bam: softrock
Hari,
country Hari from the yellow schoolbus with the South Carolina
plates
screaming HARINAM: Aging Woodstockers passing on the myths,
the Vietnam sitins, the peace and love legends to children, saried and
guitared and making dedications to great Krishna. Hari Bol, Hari Bol—a
TorontoIsland Woodstock sanitized by India a vegetarian feast, a
dance for Krishna and
afterwards a cigarette among camouflaging Canadian spruces, the
African
Krishna elder sitting on a rock alongside an ageing Swami
Eurowoman
overlooking such a placid inlet of the lake, in the shade of weeping
willows —you are convinced that Krishna himself is here. There is no
question philosophy and philosophy and the saffron robe crowned
by a stetsonlooking straw hat, a handcarved walking stick: an African
elder's presence unruffled by rhythm & blues: Hari Bol Hari Bol Hari
Bol Hari Bol.

And why could we only pick our way through the old Indian men
and
women, lying on strawmats on the tramped grass like dogs taking a
rest:

51

walk where you may I'm tired, and here the food's—well it's free and
filling.
A bone from the master: that shaven man who rambled at the mike
of mahamantra and yatras and yantras: all bhakti and ignorance of
our
history—the little yearning for Prabhupadha a dangerous
thing…navigate
the stroller to the bookstand run by the chineselooking Krishna: the
in-house-press a goldmine for the great founder's preachings,
teachings
translations, commentaries: Bhagavadgita-As-It-Is—how it was
another
myth. HariNam, Vietnam, rock n' roll, the King and I Elvis lookalike

Rushdie, eyes pulled wideback in a satan cartoon illustration
smirking;
if there was excommunication in Hinduism or blasphemy or fatwah
this would be a time. We could only clutch our selves, walk away
to the sand, spread our blanket in the shade of the marsh willows
get away from the bash: Moses having gone to the mountains must
come down. EuroKrishnas strumming the gander for the golden
eggs—
not merely palaces, departed Maharishi. In the tent behind the
freefood
kitchen, Indian women slice greenred watermelons and Indian men
serve
food—service to Krishna is service to god: like coolies cutting cane
and
weeding canerows in a time there weren't weedicides—the master in
the
Plantation House tending his accounts, or someone else's wife,
daughter…

Those tough ancestral women's Friday drink at the women's
pre-wedding
rite-of-bride-passage before the wedding night, those callused hands
now
straws drumming the dholak and twirling the night sky in dance and

laughter
out-twinkling stars. And some socialworker-anthropologist turned promoter
(of himself) recording: *dhis time nah lang time, dhis time nah lang time
dhis nah daybeforetime—langtime gattam English maanja now you gattam
'Merican*...folksong sooner to become prophecy than anyone knew.

We watched the EuroAmerican youths leave the Indian boy in the shade
with their bags, and head to the cool water, watched the straggler girl come
from behind and kick off sandals: pink toenails, even pinker toes, and sit
with him awhile, coax him—something happening   in the quietude
in the sindhur-dusk-sunshine, an indigo sky broken   in the distance
by the bellied sails of yachts: the girl awkwardly tucking the unlit cigarette
back into the pack, back into the backtrousers pocket. An evening raag
on bansuri, and gopis coming out into a lovescented evening...
finally joining the group on the water's edge, their song unsung and sung.

We remembered. And we could only dust the sand from our blanket
pack up this one unexpressed touch on the seawall of another shoreline
another dusk when you brought us food and we feasted, all this huff
nothing.   Nothing. The baby now snoring softly in the canopied
stroller.

LAKE SIMCOE

(Anne and the Bengali celebration, Kalibari Anandamela)

And there, suddenly, turning off the highway and stopping at the
entrance, it is. And we think of the lake's cool water and the sand at
the bottom. Only an hour out of Toronto you say! It is the
campground and trailer park I didn't expect—and your ghost—Anne
of the Canadian Atlantic coast, coming to Toronto to complete an MA
in English. Or somewhere the makings of a novel, scribbled poems of
despair and love and hope. *You don't know the half of it. You with your
Indian calm and equanimity and being male. That man I loved
a psycho. Freedom, freedom only in a word! And my doctor—the one you
note on those monthly cheques and payments when we try to reconcile my
statements!—that doctor wanting permission to write a book on my case. O
you're a sweetie. I did read A Passage to India—saw the movie too! A real
sweetie—couldn't we have met earlier!—a balm to have you listen because
you want to, not because I am paying!* That March, snow still on the
ground after a falsethaw weekend, they found you and your lover's
mother. Charred in the scorched camper in the park, this park!—as
you feared—he got you finally. And no one listened. Except me and
that shrink you paid handsomely to violate you. And why did I have
to come so close to death again in your indigo eyes? Courage we
lacked! To leave. Say goodbye to certain lives, venture out into the
unknown like our hardy ancestors: yours to cold Newfoundland in
the North Atlantic, and mine to hot Guiana in the South Atlantic. Our
lives touched by the same water, unknowingly. And here in the
bumper to bumper line to the park I am asking—are there any
markers with your name? A mother, sister, relative grieving—Anne
who was flesh now statistic for lobbying groups...

We drive past. Past the trailerpark—"Kalibari Anandamela" the hand
drawn sign at the gate "Kalibari Anandamela" in a Bengali script we
know and don'tknow. Something about a goddess Kali
happy/blissful mela—a happy blissful ancient Indian fair. We didn't
come for this. We are hearing this, seeing it for the for time.And yet a
memory. Was there a Bengali ancestor! It was in the Bay of Bengal,
from Calcutta in the Indian ocean that our ancestors boarded for that

seavoyage to British Guiana. That water in the Indian ocean
connected too to the Atlantic. But we pass the sign, and head for the
water's edge—wade in to our knees in cold clear water exposing a
silent film of minnows dancing through our calves: out to that island
that could be one of Essequibo's—boats sailing past the narrow pier
littered with teenage fishermen, boys wanting to learn early, the
patience for cruelty, the patience for game. Our first dip is finished.
We are towelled and reclothed. But those forecast thunderstorms not
appearing. So lucky lucky lucky. But a humidex you don't want to
know as we circumnavigate the park, leaving the shoreline. This we
can finish tomorrow, and this we can't. A regular paradox-er or
Upanishad-er depending on interpreter's worldviews —poems
should be more compact and not so seemingly damned simple that
every Jack and Jill could follow and feel they are poets
too—you see and turn away from the woman in a red flotsam of a
bikini pointed skyway over her partner, submerging her tongue in
his throat. Untanned buttocks vulgar only in your mind:
intertextuality drowned by laughter and shouts of a decidedly Indian
kind. What would Tagore say; let me translate Sant Kabir for
humankind? We pluck a green apple from a laden tree, drink from
the water fountain...examine the ancient church nearby, overlooking
a cemetery and the big rocks on which we rest, the faint trail we
follow to the treed cliff edge so we come suddenly, very suddenly to
the drop where birds are preening on rocks below, green with algae;
a ring of mocking maples and the three girls packing up their day in
bags: *And we must teach our daughters this bonding and they must teach
their daughters continuity*—yes we

smell you India before we hear you again in Bengali laughter, before
we see the richly textured red silk saris lighting up the deep green
clearing— a sweet sweet scent of curry! And back at our table
overlooking the water we pack our sandwiches away—dissatisfied.
How many of our splashes dissipate energy. This is another day at
another beach until another whorl of saris settle on that long narrow
pier near the fishing boys, and look on supremely calm: we have
learnt well of the great Rabindra lost in contemplation for hours on a
Bengali river. What this makes us yearn for, apart from a copy of his
Gitanjali, what we really want, a hundred kilometers from Toronto, is

55

food, real food. Not bread and cheese, and butter and all that mustard and… A taste of the curry in the air—even here we cannot run away from our history. But we didn't come for this for any of this! Anne, an Indian gathering—a thirst of curry! A taste of ourselves.

REPORT

Two stars already out in this dream-indigo
midsummer sky—not another of those hazy, hot
days when we must set the airconditioner
and the fan—thinking if skin touch skin. I
a little chill and bearing it in silence, you
comfortable. And does it matter? We have just
returned from a downtown hospital—and the
glare of a pigtailed-dreadlocks-in-a-quilted-head's
eyes following our crossing to the parked car
stays with us, not the hospital stench of death.

Midsummer evenings you will remember always—
In that time when remembrance rules—that time
for summer camp farewells and promises: next
summer then. Or that desire for more immediate
tomorrows, that time for those poems half the
critics skewered, half loved—all lovers loving
content displacing some lovely turn of phrase
and yet that too an utterance anchored
in cosmology, metaphors as laden as that pear
tree in a private garden where no one should
have the key except blind January. If May
were here again in this more-like-fall air
along a forefinger lake. Two days into a week
of goodbyes. We can turn the clock's arms
forward, back to a certain time. The scents
of hair just so—the same—well sweeter

and this essence. That new school of hybridity
a camp of loveless, lovelost, loveunrecalled
soulsno Bhabha, Derrida et al—no name
dropping remember. Yes, another baby on the way
extending the parameters of closeness…and this
another wonderfully young night for skywatchers.

Those two stars we talk about now joining others
in a summer's day still refusing to fade. A marvel
we never had time to ingest—or so it seemed
because we had the rest of two lifetimes. Ah yes
the apples are yet green on the trees. As green
as last year's or the year before. And there
should be time to stand under the flaming fall
beech tree—fingers entwined in that collector's
cup, downturned above our heads
and rimmed with stars—in what will always be
a southern, tropical sky.

BATTERY PARK

Circling exhaustion, and then someone pulls out
the shouts of *there there there:* playing Manhattan's
dice game—parking. Is it worth it? A chorused yes
we are lucky darkness covers everything: distracting
debris on the sand of another time we once visited
with parched peanuts on warm nights. An ocean which
would nurture Omeros, raging or calm, clucking like
hens after laying eggs in henhouses or among tree
roots on bare sand. And what was so satisfying
in those dark nights? No streetlamps. And that was
just fine, smoothing over the saltsandvines' jagged
march along that old Dutch seawall—a spider's webs
clutching runaway papercups and paperplates, and if
you looked carefully, squashed condoms: West Indian

poets who divide their time between Miami and Boston
and Toronto and New York—the East Village, say, but
write about those Indies, or Africa, or a Europe's old
countryhouse of another century where the transported
"black prince" makes earl or duke; a way in the world
—five daughters becoming five country gentlewomen
and in these fictions you notice how all these servants
served England well; Empire! how all these a-ordinary
men came from distant lands' royalties. The queen the
queen the queen is dead—long live the Empress
of India!—and though she never set foot here
you are assured this is a copy of some such park
in old, oceanencirled Britain—island to island: the
linden trees from Germany, the ginkgos from China, the
invisible cannons pointing out to sea from a visible
twin towers; old Britannia ruling the South China
seas no longer, the July 1 handover approaching
despite Patton's last stand supported by a White House
not wanting to celebrate: the Sioux might want all its
lands back, or the Iroquois…but the China trade…This
is not the dragon's last dance: next year Macao, and next
more of Tibet, tankshod over the monasteries and Lamas
the made-in-China (by American firms) stamp on toys and
gadgets increasing the made-in-America films and poems
and fictions. Ah yes it is getting chill in the latenight
air for the kids we forgot in another time joying in the
past-bedtime and the Diwali lit ships passing through the
Demerara bar into ocean laden with bauxite, highgrade ore
sugar, sugarcane spirits… It is a long walk back
in the silence to the parked car. If our parents did this
for us! Ma gone without goodbye—no hug or kiss we could
ever remember. Daddy in less than a blink yet allowing
me to close his eyes. Our sleepy kids filling that void.

FROM CONVERSATIONS IN NEW YORK CITY

Churki: this ceremonial tuft of hair shaking
from my shaved head I bear proudly
from Demerara to Ganges to The Big Apple.
This symbol from the ritual for the departed
is my karma—man good to see yuh good to see
yuh in the land of the brave and the bold
and the ready con at every corner. I feel
at home. Well wuk is wuk—I pumping gas only
the cold—yes yes Canada colder. So everybody
say. Man but look at my awards: fellowships
at Yaddo, Miami, The Guyana Prize. My work
staged at York. And dhem Guyanababu jealous.
One coolie poet—yuh know who a mean—say
I makeup mih awards, another reporting dhat
I say that when I land at Toronto airport
a white woman kidnap me, saying she come
to collect me for the conference. Put me up
in a airport hotel room for four days and
fucked me and loved me and when she went to
the toilet I escape and call my uncle!—
that is what he said I seh when I return to
Guyana and you probably hear this story
making the rounds in Toronto. Like if
people in Guyana stupid! Rumours and if I
ketch that bhai who said so I wring his
neck. They can't handle this success nor
this churki I wear proudly from Demerara—
my mother dead and yet lives. I must
visit India, return to Guyana someday but
I'm here to take on America and will, watch
me bhai...but upstate—ah there was a
wonderful white woman, a wonderful place
man I wrote and wrote and wrote—those
rolling hills, stacked hay, frogs in ponds
toads in trees calling, mingling with the
kiskadee's songs... Write me when you get
back, keep in touch—and don't forget I
don't pretend I'm Hindu, I let my churki fly...

59

THE CANADIAN NATIONAL EXHIBITION

We look automatically skyward
for the cablecar high above.
Once we travelled softly
over the crowd, unchilled and alone,
fingers locked, calves xed—all these
lights of the city's endofsummer dusk
reflecting off the lake—dots in that
other light warming fingers tonight
and long ago confluencing.

We stretch
our lives to limits and so must stretch
language. It is the end of our night's
day, long past the children's bedtimes.
The hot August night hotter
with all these lights on Ferris wheel
merry-go-round, rollercoaster, cartoon
characters blaring stock-theme-songs
Unchanged from other childhoods
on other continents—these lights, those
stars, this space a galaxy: excursions
to gaming tables and corporate techno
booths softly softly selling softly
an odyssey north from the southern
juggernaut spot on—Lord Jagganauth

The cosmic spirit mocked by colonizing
lords as the evil heathen now coming home
to roost—the cock doing his diddle
well, his chicks named from India—Euro
America casting doubt north of the 42nd
parallel. What is Canadian about Canada—
a spirit circumscribed by snow? Watch this

Flare of lights outcoloured by a sindhur
sun settling into a lake we share—the

Imax bought by entrepreneurs down south
now a US thing—a case in Indian courts
where corporateamerica copyrights neem—
our birthright: a Sanskrit word, Ayurvedic
wonderplant—not margosa—that now
no Indian firm should use this name

This Sanskrit name: neem poem, my bitter
sweet neem pen on a neem page—so sue me
for my poetry book NEEM, my fiction NEEM
and we can go to Hollywood with a Plummer
and a Fox, an Ackroyd and a Candy
stretching your hand from my British
Oxford English: that word from Sanskrit

Khanda—sweet sweet sweet candyfrost
the kids stuff in mouths and laugh
at sticky foodcolouring on each other's
lips: Candy going to school here
in Scarborough by the lake of the famous
bluffs. Scarborough by the English sea
side. Today we celebrate India's 50th

Two hundred and forty thousand
nobody asked: these thrice shipwrecked
throwbacks to an indentured century
from South America or Fiji or South
Africa's Capetown Coolie; what Michael
Caine movie would have him sitting
in an Indian moviehouse playing Raj
Kapoor's "Anari"—fool fool fool?

The children gamboling in the new
airconditioned Ex—building curving
like Pearson's Terminal Three, and
we have a minute, two, three to sit
in the night air and follow
the laser lights animating clouds

61

Superman or Winnie-the-pooh, bugs
bunny coming to life under the art
of northerners sailing south like Vikings
—let Columbus take the credit—
Chinese sailors landing on the California
coast a thousand years previously; a Shatner
sailing into starwars starspace legend

We will hold our tongues
in our timeswallowing
energysapping domesticity and look down
our strong noses—even like those
Nova Scotians descended from the Civil
War underground railway flight to Freedom

Tight lips tougher than any cowboy
Hollywood bravado or bluster. And what
is Canadian? Our kids, someone murmurs—
our kids! Time to get the joying children to bed
to dream of what that Canadian means. And we
exit the parking lot neem neem neem neem neem…

QUEEN WHO WOULD BE KING

No swords these days
and so only to say
those who live by the media's
flash and instant—or tomorrow's
FrontPage photos die by them—
this tragedy thinking you could
manipulate cameras to become
queen of king of hearts.

But was there time to die
in the glare of searchlights
and wreckage-extraction workers:

in the operating room; sometimes
gifted hands return life?
Light setting on an Empire.

Red English eyes outside
Kensington Palace, their queen
—what queen!—dead.
And that very medium blamed
shifting blame to a secluded Balmoral
memorial. Joy is private, sexcapades
with dildo private. But not grief
of anointed boys.

Ma dying slowly. Eight, and we couldn't
afford even tears. Not through wakenight
rumdrinking, not through the cortege,
not through aunts and uncles weeping—
not for months, not for years after.

If you eat cake don't want us
all to eat cake too. Give us roti.
To grieve publicly or privately
over death unbecomes these last
brahminborns of the west. Leaders
should have composure when others
call for blood from Westminster—

Poor Charlie Kilting a Scots countryside
quietly and teaching a strength
he should have shown years ago
Camilla Parker Bowles yump ki yump
ki yump. And not suffer the mice
saying whom to marry when.

Shut down the palace, demolish the tower
open a shrine on another little isle.
Admission prices later!
If you will, if you must quote
that scripture of India: Bhagavadgita.

63

As far as we know—those days
there were no cameras.
Even Siddartha Gautam had affairs
—didn't divorce his wife
yes, deserted her—
before heading for Buddhahood.

Tender fingering in a Paris hotel
—O heart of hearts!—infinitely
better sounding than sex. Our mothers
have every right to be more concerned
about their whole. Let the priests
look after their souls.

I.

quibbling with its fall
we were starting
a whole new life—
that inscription

on slate soon erased
supplanted
by other words
and loves
and lives

MARTIN CARTER

Forgive me if ever I came
to stand before you
in your own worn boots
thinking I brought myself.

Today I come unshoed
and lotus my legs
and wait to watch your language.

II.

Those raucous bluejay calls
and midSeptember sun turning
behind the overcastcold plotting
with earlycolouring maple leaves

Some presence intoning
summer's done done done

But it wasn't always. Once
under midoctober sun
under a fuller flush of leaves
under a lip of water falling...

III.

And if such time could come again
O love O love O love

65

IV.

High over that gorge
walking over a bridge
up stonesteps in a hill
across a museum's balcony
pieces looking out to lake
holding the tips of spruces
marking an unhurried sailor
expectant in the waves—
if we exit now
late lunch
and all which matters
—on such trips and yet—
in the waiting
in the drapedin room.

IT IS NEVER EASY TO SAY GOODBYE

Snow which slipped us
into guardrail, which came
and will again, and burnt
our faces in cold night winds
dribbled tears from eyes. And ice
which made us swear why why why.

Land in which the apple bloomed
and ripening, fragranced air
your leaves turn shades of lips
falling falling falling.

Decorating a velvet floor—
this grass is always greenest
before it looses greenness. Yet
just a little thaw in spring
catches fires of chlorophyll.

May among the wine-route blooms
July atop the lemonade falls
the magic of a northern forest
celebrating ancient stone etchings.
All we enjoyed without our making.

And how difficult it is
O how difficult it is
to say goodbye again—
another land you hate
and learn to love and hate

and love. And every time, and every
time it gets harder harder harder

V.

Such words which meant a world
and noworld. Such innocence
from not-so-innocents. To believe
somewhere someone whose goodness
could bring out our own—gloss
such tiny things—the way you tossed
down refreshment, the space money
preserves—*youu understand
don't youu?* What it is to sail
past that beacon—forty—
unnoticeably. To be young and loved
again. Have hope for the future.
Dine in trendy restaurants among
well mannered people casting
oblique-est of approving glances—
understand? Such a time such a time
a town a place. Trees. So many shades
of cheeks laboured in the mirror
of leaves. A cool conducive
to caresses back in the room—a few

days for the remainder of oncoming
winter. Memories which planning makes—
we could never tell for sure. Scores
of monarch butterflies hovering around
the lakeshore before the long flight
south to a different foliage; reason
not yet catching up to the returning
generations, recurring journeys, obsessions.

VI.

These are those familiar sounding
youu can tell mee—eyes widening
and pupils sticking questions—
how the grass is greenest
when leaves are the shades
of eyeliners and mascara. And that
colour you brush on cheeks, apply
on lips, smoothing over cracks
in relationships. Words, like that
solitary bench in the middle
of that green summer field set up
for use. And now deserted.

WAITING

So we travel these hundred
kilometers, take such care noting
places visited, even laugh
at the bulldog (you're right, I am
no Gandhi) of a pipesmoking
Prime Minister's paraphrased comments:
*the most scenic Saturday afternoon
drive in the world.* Along the river
to Niagara-on-the-lake. This most
Euro of Canadian towns purchased

in chunks by that millionaire Chinese
lady reversing Empire—
make more millions and let journals
stew other pages of discontent
or resentment or defence we cannot see
all those white picket fences, clipped
lawns, houses laid back in yards like
perfunctory sex, the mansion fitted
with Demerara shutters ringed by
a wooden walkaround verandah. And this
the first time we're making this trip
at night sitting on the old colonial
seawalls supervised by ghosts of Dutch
and British architects as foreign
ships negotiate the Demerara channel
and those tricky sandbars lengthening
with the tide and effluence leaping
from the very soul of a continent.
Centuries of southern rainforests
wearing along the edges, rocks
and loose gravel billowing like
a dancer's skirt. Deliberate sightings
underneath. And having come back
the revolving tower rising and falling
over this riot of tinseltown lights
not reaching those rundown streets
we negotiated at noon; and you wouldn't
stop, not even for gas. Get to the inn
unpack, relax, sort out the itinerary
we owe the kids, even-in-the-womb,
everything evenly: that one going
east and north into the Laurentian
mountains, this one west to the falls' edge
across the rainbow bridge to Goat Island
—all the while thinking of Panther Key
in the Florida straits—and that old
pirate (he met Napoleon!) nearly hung
in Havana; his missing goats devoured

—so he said to his rumed audience
out for laughs, hoping for something—
there being no radio or TV—even the next
hurricane rather than their ordinariness:
all those pieces composed in heads
awaiting transcription. If there is
time, and the sameness editors demand.

SOUFRIERE

Letter from nowhere, crossing the blue
Atlantic: how you finally understand
my ache and anger—my pain
of exile. Montserrat a tiny island
nursing your five hundred year history
up in ash—the volcano a sore
belching a planet's rebellion
and in a few hours your town
gone: those buildings
of a British empire building
you cursed—gone, those
plantations' echoes of shackled Africa
and bubbly childhoods loved
and hated gone. One day a home
the next none.

You were luckier my friend, luckier.
Day by day for twenty years we saw
ours erased before our eyes: home
and history and existence. Our pride
stolen, our folklore appropriated.
The right to be second or third class
citizens branded on our foreheads
for all the world. Our new enclaves
laughed at expatriate functions.
A triumph of slavery and Africa. But
following our hearts and our Gandhi's

tiny voice, we do not write for Nobel
prizes—for any prizes. To be
community's conscience even though
our children starve.

But to govern my India into the ground!
And to laugh, how you laughed! And mocked
my references to race. But didn't
during Civil Rights or in deep Dixie—
you from Africa too. No this has nothing
to do with race and colour! Unless
the British placed lava-boilers
in the mountain. But I wasn't there.
And in all those poems of loss
you must now write: smells of sulphur
and burnt earth, the colours of ash
and lava, is it like blood? O dear
fellow exile, is it like blood
the same everywhere?

ORANGE-JUICE FLAME

This time last year you weren't talking
and barely standing alongside the sofa
wondering what was all this fuss with
these flames in baked earthen vessels.
And you were to invent a colour, a whole
vocabulary. The wordsmith out already.
What use telling you poets are poorly
remunerated for their poetry—if at all.

We named those clay vessels for you
diya, diiyaa, diya memorying a time
we went to mudbanks, kneaded earth
we carved, smoothed. Our mixture
transformed into earthen vessels for

71

oil or ghi, and cotton wicks we lit
to welcome the festival of lights, all
returned to mudbanks. Sacred soil back
to sacred soil—ancient instincts
of the receivers of land's bounty:
orchards of oranges and a certain breeze
rustling citrus leaves—those forked
branches which didn't pull away
their seats from fruit bunches.
Not freshplucked on tongues, these past
months all you saw was, "minute maid"
"old south"…from concentrate or not
in frozen boxes or anemic transparent
plastics. A sickly looking yellow
you know as your measure: orangejuice
butterfly! The proud monarch heading
for Mexico renamed. Orangejuice leaves
falling from maples—and they even
joked during purnima, orangejuice moon.

And today the orangejuice fire
in the orangejuice diyas of Diwali—
the orangejuice festival of lights.

Yesterday that world map on the doctor's
wall evoked one word among astonished
adults: India! Forgetting we have
been here before. Wordmendering.

DADDY

Nothing like any piano—
like any grand piano:
that small mandolin
hung from a little nail
in the opentopped bedroom
typical of those tropics.

A silence for years
after she departed.
The strings green in places
the frets dull, dust competing
with mosquito dung and time
and gnawing desire.

What of those sounds
which had enraptured her—
and all those other women
and men of their time?

Fingers quivering—those eyes
leaking memory: *the years and rum—*
joints stiff—I don't know...
Eyes lighting, fingers dancing
start with these notes
this raag...did he ever stop?
Raags! And we thought...
If pens could play
such mandolins
if only our pens could pluck
such intoxicating mandolin raags!

THE MOUNTAINS ARE ALWAYS NORTH

Rising out of water
on brushed slate
on the quay in Lonsdale market
abeer-red paint suddenly splashed
by an excited glove gesticulating
poet to painter to poet:
the catamaran skimming Burrard Bay
in minutes—front front and back
front: seabus terminal to foothills—
if there were nobobyelse, nobobyelse

but those peaks and us in mists
in rivulets of snow in cracks of ages—
O those so female, nippled mountains
and Shiva lost descending—to a stranger:
avoid that strip between Chinatown
and the water, Public Transit's fine,
and remember— if you're lost in Vancouver
the mountains are always north.

OLD YEAR'S OR NEW YEAR'S EVE

Old heaters in old houses
hissing, or like rusted sitar
strings bursting—but there is heat
yet on this cold night. And silence's
certain music when all's abed
and the ball spinning, twinkling
on the descent of another Times
Square moment when all the world
watches—if an island's a world
hyperbolic broadcasters in an
hyperbolic land—paper floating
down to be picked up
later today—or tomorrow
yesterday's joys in a warmer land
if we could remember just one time
when we might have been together
—you all of six months. Horsing
around, toygun sulphur hanging
on to the waiting to move
into that new house—

If you could know her as we did—
wonderful mother in a short happy life
that never was—for you
the measure of all my gifts

through all our too short meetings—
the spaces in between growing brighter
in this ball descending
and the disappearance. Until next year
then, until next time, dear brother.

THIS NORTHERN SKY

In this sky—far too high up
the surgical lines of walls
are creamed and lighting
a night measured by clocks'
precise ticking. No trace
of those who went before
no creaking floorboards echoing
previous occupants' idiosyncrasies
of footfalls inadequately muffled
by carpets from India or Turkey
or sputtering heaters fighting
vainly against homeowners' pride—

possession. Keep it cool
keep the energy bill down
just dress warmer in the fall
this winter of our new year—
it's okay to splurge on fairy lights
Christ! everyone else in Queens
does—on the outside. What people
see or hear matters! Echoes of cars
mythologizing a citywhichneversleeps
too far away in a colder
more northern suburb devoid
of the too steep, too narrow stairs.

Or the charactered dwellings
on which we slipped in nani's

log-slabbed downstairs smoothed over
with cardboard. Gill's beer garden
and billiards table across the Cummings
Canal—if we punched out knots
in the wood, the players visible—
clasping those long tapered sticks
late into the tropical night;
the latrine behind, a part of the
treescape of huge genips—
The cowpen still smelling of ages
or Ahirs herding cattle
on the Gangetic plain—the godboy
Krishna chateying the buttermilk
from his fingers. That very finger
with which, later, he would hold up
Goberdhan mountain to shelter
his cowpeople relatives from
the vengeful rain of the Aryan
thundergod Indra—henceafter
demoted to demigod: what they did

At Easter; daddy and mommy's mamoos
on the floor of the swept cowpen
still smelling deliciously of Gangetic
dust, framing kankawas—kiteflying
an ancient art on that ancient plain—
and when an inevitable loop burst
or tangled in those tall palms
more awe than tears watching
fragments of Barbados paper, remnants
of Walcott's Nobel vase so easily

Remoulded. Hybridity unheard of, or
the broken minds of the midnight authors;
creolize creolize creolize: having never
known of the midnight birthing blue light
crossing the river in Vasudeva's basket

In our fathers' hands every creation

76

an original, a pure delight of Ganga
or Jamuna coasting off the Demerara
singing into the Atlantic—what matters
in name? And yet all waters of all rivers
meeting off maps, off novels, off epics
on paper—unless you live too high up
in the north, in the toocold too long.

HILL OF FIRE

whenever cane is ripe
there is deep red flame—
flame like a smouldering hill of fire...

MARTIN CARTER

Old thunders silenced so rapidly
there isn't any time for grieving.
Now we understand
the equanimity of undertakers;
those two gravediggers
sitting on a nearby tomb
and sipping rum
straight from the flatty:
the pandit uttering mantras,
performing last rites, some
relative or adult familyfriend
offering a clump of wet earth
to pelt on your coffin sliding
into a sceptictanklookingcell.

Nothing meant anything
to eightyearolds, mommy; little
yogis or that Indian conditioning
to control—much more control
than those legendary British lips
blubbering outside Buckingham palace!

I didn't weep. Not a single tear
not even in private—not then not
now as these poets' bodies shrink
inevitably; worms or rather, fire.

So no cementfresh graves today
but blazing pyres—from afar in
snowedin Toronto—celebrating
the crackle of coconut shells
on these seashores of those worlds
buried behind and yet baggaged in
those verses of Resistance
and Affinity and Succession
and Mortality dipped
in that Ponce's Fountain
(the heat the heat the heat!)
that Florida Fountain of unold.

READING THE JOY OF WRITING

(after Wislawa Symborska)

Searching the jammed cricket stands
on the far side—with binoculars—
slowly: all these great—supposedly—
poets' collected/selected for an image
or a rhythm or a rasa might ignite
fingers, burn these long gaps of unpoem.
Nothing. The players gather around the
watercart—selected—backing the relentless sun.

Such a glorious day for cricket!
Out with the food, uncork the spirits
of sugar cane juice! Lower the powerful
glasses, easing the strain on eyes.
And there in the pavilion Shiva turns

around—just infront! No. It isn't the strong
white rum, or the killer smooth
tenyear old, cured in the casks left
behind by British planters, chasing
the cutters after a day in the field
to Ramayana in Fiji or Trinidad or BG

Yet Shiva winks—he might have been
telling that story of Raghubir
to Parvati—and waves from that row
right ahead, and ups on one foot
and dances in this long dry spell
like, you know, the Nataraja himself.
And we get up drunkenly. And dance too.

ROUGE RIVER-ON-THE-LAKE

Those grey pebbles
on the inner beach, puddles
of cementlooking water
and all we cared about
were the butterflies
and geese. And yes, those
two tagged trumpeter swans—
one on the far side
of the marsh. The older kids
back to school, impatient
to be older—were you
listening only to the
cadences, or the boyfriend
girlfriend talkity-talk?

If time could find eternity
there! Those kayaking legs
of girls come back
to light the sunshine;

the canoe club's makeshift
containerhouse open—there
was a fire—the basketball
ring resounding, thousands
of monarch butterflies
resting on the lakeshore
before crossing the lake
into New York state, geese
basking in sunshine
caught between a late fall
and a late summer: will we
see you next year, will we

Or your descendants even?
Three generations, four?
It isn't that you don't care.
You have grasped eternity
in your little limbs
the sweetness of uncertainty
and mortality. What will
next year be like? But, dear
child, never let it be said
we didn't run this way. Once
—an ancestral memory
like the butterfly's.
A Gangetic breeding ground.

PASSENGERS ON THE VANCOUVER ISLAND FERRY

One decade on an eastern lake. A
land which hips gently; long curves
loved except in snow storms. Perhaps
even Algonquians and Iroquois
came from elsewhere. Helped along
by firesticks. Then another place.

Moving. The ferry threading
such islands rising out of Brahma's
soup to mountains taking breath
away—sundown all around. If
we'd only known before what's it
like to come home—Shiva dancing
in red rays pierced by peaks
in clouds, in epics by Indian
authors who are not Indian: Rushdie
Roy...looking like Anne of the West,
Anne of the Pacific—that ocean too
connected to the Atlantic—*just so I can
understand my Indian husband more! I'm
just coming back from my monthly trip
to my Victoria therapist. Some things
you talk to your spouse about
some things you talk to strangers
about—if you're a successful
entrepreneur as I am. You know—*

*but one needs to talk. Among such
mountains! my husband's from your
ancient land. My father made me the son
he always wanted...your bus? Yes
goodbye. If we come your way again—
I'll read your books. Your name, titles?
Ah yes, but these watered foothills,
these cloudkissed peaks is all the home
I'll ever know. Want to know—and my
husband's land.* She went back
to The God of Small Things.

NIBBLING AT RESENTMENT

It comes sometimes—what use
lying—amidst the deadfall
of domesticity, in the gurgling
of the baby—sunshine bubbling
down a winter drainpipe;
amidst the neon lights
in the mall: how we practise
this infant's voice, tease
a variation from a shriek…

And how to listen carefully
to the weave of coconut fronds
in a dawn breeze; the whisper
of a shadow on swept concrete.

Yes, so it comes, nibbling
at resentments: I need my space
and you need yours; wearing
thin, that bud of hate
those castes of schedules. But
there is laughter
in our hearts today—
transmitted from the baby's.

MIDWINTER

No matter what you say
about language and imagery
or lack thereof.
No matter that you see
the truck sliding downhill
inches from your windscreen
or Olympians jumping
the snowed skies of Hakuba

for gold, or—except for
conifers—trees minus green,
the gray Toronto sky—no
matter what you say, when
Devi laughs on baby's face
who needs groundhog day?

BLACK MONDAY:
GEORGETOWN, JANUARY 12 1998—FROM AFAR

Even after walking over
seas and setting in snow
far away, far far away
who wouldn't let us go—
labaria spittle striking
eyes—so we would not see
'64. History rewriting itself

in looted stores of Indians and
the rapes—and who would report
and who would not, the stigma,
and the beating of he (the Indian
businessman) learning support
of those at the cuffy monster
not enough: house slave leaders
busy raping captive Dutch women

the beginning and end
of the revolution—rabble rousing
under that Godzilla thing
clasping—is that a severed penis
—what the Dutch infantry did after?

The only qualification
for a beatingrapinglooting
being Indian. Knowing now

how the Ashkenazi felt
in the pogroms—fiddler
on our roofs dancing: let jhalls
become Mahabharata chakras—

no western mystical symbol
but a hightec force—spiritualism!
No loverboygodboy fluting
sunset ragas. Yes, I've run away
if only to remind you
you are not a coward
you are not a coward
you are not a coward—

ask those heads-of-black
governments across the CARIB(sic)
bean sea: where were you
when your brothers ruled
with fascist fists, allblack
military units; Tutsis and Hutus—
if this be Africa…

Remind you of the Warsaw Uprising
of the 1857 "mutiny." Not, if only
we were in the army! but that too.
And if not like profligate
holocaust movies, stories, books
the pen the pen the sword

LETTER

Kicking sand
in an afternoon sunshine
and drinking
ocean air on lotioned skin
such textured calves
and thighs hiding string

84

bikinis in cleavages—
or a poetry reading in
a South Florida summer's night
moonshine on muscles of Amazons

warming a northern winter dusk—
but a licked stamp
a licked edge of an envelope
where moisture never dries
now DNA knows why
that fragranced messenger
missive was love anticipated
not unentirely unknowingly.

So no email please no email.

A CITY

"Hell is a city much like Port-of-Spain"
if you are as double honed
as Walcott: Europe burnt
by Africa or political correctness.
I could tell you
of that city of my birth
or those black gangs
pouncing on those not-so-black
people with straight hair—
the professor from South Africa
writing "Dear cousin cousin"—
you know India came
from the vagina of Africa
"Just look at your Dravidian south."

Black gangs beating and burning
and looting not-so-black businesses.
Is this the insecurity of kids

85

in the seedier parts of Los Angeles—
that City of Angels; the Korean
shopkeeper holding a shotgun
near his cash register—you blame
him? All those flames
witnessed in the sixties.

Thirty years of torment. Another exile—
paki paki paki, wheels screaming
in the whitenesslike underground.
Toronto city of cold or New York's
black holes—some Harlem the Dutch
couldn't dream or some Bronx
some Brooklyn-raucous-carnival
rousing the Hasidim. What could I
steal or burn or loot or mug
in the Haitian section of Miami—
blackbirds on every tree at a Biscayne
corner: introduced European starlings.

And turning another page
into another century, we come
upon one we left behind—those
not-so-browns ripping storefronts
they didn't build, explosions—
O those explosions in pre-election
India when after the Muslims
and Christians—the British
and Portuguese—the Italian
Gandhi is poised to rule!
But hell—though I could not tell you
nor could Naipaul: they would
burn him too—hell in the Americas
is being not black enough
or white enough for Lucy's descendants.

If you subscribe to that theory!

DEIFYING JUAN PONCE DE LEON

Live heroes and streets
in every other Florida city
travelling through space.
This is the present, the time
deification usually takes
place—in the post mortem
by sympathetic pens. Captain
Cook in the south Pacific
returning a mastbroken ship.
Would not natives know
gods can fly even with broken
wings? That gods do not die
from dagger wounds? Ah Ponce
Ponce Ponce—your Spanish
mythmakers! The natives would
not even let you land beyond
the beach: strutting like
a turkeycock in platearmour.
But mustn't elbows move
and neck; your adam's apple
pierced and letting blood
spill on the Florida sand
on shipboard, on retreat
in Havana: all these Cubans
rafting. You can't miss
how many under, how many
made it and later galloping
soonantiquated gaseating horses
of the twentieth century
on a certain Castilian blvd
or street: stereos lancing
the night
        muchachos muchachas
        vaya con dios
        aay Macarena aay Macarena
        aay…

whatever it means
whatever all this means
in that oldest migration story
—natives hounded out, exiled—
who comes first goes first.

MOVING TO YET ANOTHER LAND

Glare, even with sun pushing through
creamgrey clouds—all these tiny flakes
falling in a hurry before March ends
our time in this corner of the woods, white
everywhere—even on pines and spruces
which would be greener. And eyes hurting
though the sun is not penetrating leaves
of greenheart and purpleheart and mora
down to the white sand up the Demerara
river nearby. A black creek hustling
and before the sun turns down noon
the others' hurrying, laughter receding
to the bathing logbridge—who wanting
the solitude (it was the reason
why we came) of the tiny clearing
on the hill where vision runs
to tall trees and ends in the trail.
An Arawak woman threads barefooted
with her silence of centuries
and her surety of steps; her baby
strapped infront—the lunchbag behind—
so many miles ago and trees and blue
butterflies, how many trails away
yesterday we left her husband's camp
behind: huge greenhearts falling singly
after the chainsaws, a chipping away
of branches then silence. Forest silence.
Logs to be pulled out to loggers' trucks

tomorrow or the day after. As it always
happens the great builders live elsewhere
not in this unquiet quiet with its glare
of sun on crystal sand or powdered snow:
a disjunction of sentences and paragraphs
and chapters story editors cannot see
the goodbyes again to forest sands

and now goodbye again to snow.

NEWSCASTER: "RAWANDA LAND OF..."

Land of one hundred thousand
murderers. And should we have any
sympathy with the displayed skulls?
History should not be forgotten
so soon after the killing fields
of Serbia or Pol-Pot's Cambodia
or a Japanese China or the eternal
ovens like that eternal flame
on Parliament Hill fed by gas.
A holocaust movie, book, play
a minute a day. And History should
not forget its selectiveness. Who
controls the media controls History.
What have we learnt? That all those
murderers considered their tribes
superior—like our butchers'
respectable profession on every
continent, country; to put sheep
or pig, a crop of fowl
in a predetermined henhouse to
sleep. From incubation to a tandoori
table are we lands and countries of an
hundred hundred thousand cannibals!

DENNIS STREET

Reading and rereading
your own folly in print
in little and not so little
journals—all the other dewdrops
on leaves on trees on the riverbank
brilliant and inhabitable
until the glory of a tropical sky
midmorning, drying every droplet.

And you are left with your own
folly: times and places
and people you should never
never mention—do women have
longer memories than men? This is
nothing new—or even a new way
of seeing old sores—we went

barefoot everywhere; in puddles of
the rainy season, in the huge landfill
(later to become The Housing Scheme
playfield) picking through
others' refuse for gems—for tin caps
of Pepsi or creamsoda bottles—poring
over atlases: that year they ran
that competition to make you buy
more D'Aguiar aerated drinks:

shapes of countries printed in black
under the cork linings—and you had
to collect the world. Whatever happened
to the winners? Today we still remember
all those countries whose borders
remain unchanged, fit them to continents
to peoples, to landscapes. Nothing about

sores or the fallouts. The new Health
Centre near the dump filling up quickly
the new Fire Station proud of its new
flagpoles like sentries over the blackwater
canal, and this street soon to become infamous
for the more bloody of the Jonestown murders

the ex-marine carrying out to the letter
of slit throats, the last commands of
the dead leader near his wooden
throne-in-the-bush crowned with:
those who forget the past are condemned
to repeat it. Or see yourself
in hastily scrambled books and movies.

Hollywood and the New York Publishers
seizing the day. Twenty years later—
almost—cashing in; a Canadian book
of poetry, a Wilson Harris novel
on the American follies in a far country.
Dirty white sunburnt Americans wolfing
down GuyaneseChinese food in the sun—

on a weekend pass to the city.
What must their diet have been like?
They were at least assured of food!
And all that bush and silence—
the concrete jungle of Los Angeles
far away. Having come a long way
ourselves and not knowing if anyone
is following as we rewrite our memories:

those who cannot forget the past
are condemned to rehash it. Or in wonder
exclaim (instant fame and money, like
the New York quickie books:
Guyana Massacre) *you hold our worst*
buut pisach—our worst ghosts from

beyond; our sweetest untranslatable

I used to live there, once!

Let nothing else be said. Nothing else.

POET TO POET

Wandering along a footpath
wrapped in the skirt
of a tropical breeze: *What if*
questions hanging in the air
like hair we have seen
ourselves naked on a pave
what trees are these
with hanging roots in air
poet to poet searching
ficus ficus—figs of India.
No these hair-roots cannot
be... Everything I—we touch
is India. *Well yes. And farewell.*

DEAR DOCTOR

And perhaps you will not laugh
now. Not that you laughed much
then. This spring's only invitation
to The Apple is to a shraad—
the death rites of that other friend
colleague who made well in America
before the cancer. Never too young!

And why all that silence
from last May to this?

I lost my pen
until today, under the mat
under the seat of that little
car you looked at disdainfully
just for a second your eyes:
that thing—the America Car!
Detroit's answer to the little
lovable fuelefficient Japanese
autos of the hip sixties and
seventies gnawing the guts of American
humble pie, Hiroshima and all—
brought you all the way from Toronto!

We are riding our silences
higher: on a hill looking out
to the Atlantic, cars anting
over the Verrazano Bridge—this
Toronto spring warmer—el nino—
than any in memory and so many
blossoms everywhere—on the woman
with the leashed dog pausing

to commend: "that is marvelous
the horticultural lesson you give
to your son." These are lilacs and
these are apple blossoms, more intense
than stars. Last week we sucked
small spice mangoes; Hindi *am*. Simple!

And you tell me what else we have
in common: not merely the tastebuds
of Bhaarat or Govapuri but touch
whether in the OR rectifying heartclogs
or the epic page—the ivory stylus
of Ganesh—how many poems since

last week the Toronto agent said
but no no no, its your voice—

you haven't quite found your voice
as yet. And yet— But let's meet! Coffee?
A beverage gifted by Ethiopia to the world
and especially to ER doctors we would
come to thank much much later.

THOSE EYES OF THE EXPORTED INDIAN BIRD

(after Suresh & Peter)

The twin peacocks on the walls
of a well in dusty Nazareth
or a paired mural in Elvis' house
from a maternal Jewish grandmother—
if we let you copyright our history
and ancestry—those now Jewish
feathers borrowed from Hind—
Solomon eager to impress Sheba:
the cock following
the Roots-in-the-Air poet
now resettled in "The Holy Land"
—Madurai or Haridwar or Varanasi?—
making love to an ancient Indian fig.

Somewhere in New York or New Delhi
an American company arguing in court
to copyright the Sanskrit *neem* —if
we let your women steal our peacocks
or vegetarianism willingly!—O but
to keep those limbs young and fatfree
cocksure or gaily cockfree; corporate
keepfit manage-missing yoga. Shiva
a US missile and this week protesting
the Indian test blasts in the Thar desert
and withdrawing the striped aid—band
aid barely concealing a nick of a part

of a part of a finger. If any more
blasts go off the consequences; those
Hindu nationalists! but France last year
joining the club easily: another Euro
cousin in the Eurovan, what? All dazzled

by the Indian tail spread to the sun
and that wily crane who said, on behalf
of the other peeved animals—a fable:
you cannot fly. But you can be taken
around the world, adopted for your
multiplication of purity: Salman
wincing and Walcott, or Harris in
his Palace of the (our) Peacock—that
original steal of Solomon focused
on the seduction; we can tell you
the exact year and port of shipping
those celebrated songs of...but those
eyes between the dash and the comma
the South American Suresh painted
for a cover—swords cartwheeling
space cartwheeling Sind or Hind or Ind.

NOT IRISH EYES

It wasn't so much, Maggie,
those Irish eyes we would see
in the morning, stuck up on the fridge
door—snapshots of the family
spread out on the Pacific coast
a sister down under. But it was
that Irish tongue taking getting used to
in the dark, rolling around the car
deliciously: let's go dountouwn
around a corner of Canada's first
Chinatown. How they poured across

95

the water! Not that alone or parking
on the bay—where was east or west
or north—driving in the dark
through the mansions on the hill
among the huge oaks—the last stand
of the English in North America—
that an Irish snicker? Parked
near the castle on the hill looking
at stars or passing through the
U of V campus; hockey night under
floodlights: not that fighting
on ice. The real thing on grass
and afterwards over tea questions:
family, fulltime occupation, age.
No I don't mind! And how we do it!
You are nearing completion
of your first collection of poems
and every time and space and winter
passing through the pages. Goodnight
goodnight goodnight lingering awake.
With morning scones for the long ferry
ride into Vancouver—farewells: if
I bring my family west. Sure. And If
you ever come east…today in Northern
Ireland, Maggie, they voted for peace.

THE WEATHER CANNOT COMPLAIN?

A false summer which began in March
finally getting its due in June
—pin these on El Nino; early fires
long droughts and elsewhere floods
floods and more…and if your cock
cannot crow, El Nino—a cold front
moving in, locking up your brains
fingers frozen in the early morning

park: tiny white butterflies whirring
by like helicopters, and the infant
chased last week by a bumble bee
remembers, must be hoisted—sight
of any flying insect—a bug is a bug
is a bug—setting off bells. Stuck
to the perimeter of the tarmac. Last
year reversed, chasing anything which
moved, tiny heels kicking up sunrays
on grass. Such blue sky of another time
and sunshine, the fingers warmed
the pages of books moving rapidly—
who says the weather cannot complain?

GETTING INTO STRIDE

Summer before summer
below lowrise-highrise
on a hill the surly man
above trash in the valley
unleashing his pitbull:
go git'em boy; these coolies
and latinolookingsounding intruders!
The kids joyfully unaware
dribble a footsoccerball across
the womenkept lawn (you don't
say such sexist thing publicly lest
languagesexistracistageisthomophobia
cops out their rage—if this wasn't
a private poetry sliding steadily
into obscurity!). Such order
and finery: lace trees; alder
sprinkling the edges of walkways—
pedestrian language—vinemaples
hemming the valley. The fire gone
with the sun behind clouds, spring

stumbling out of bed. Light jackets
and the exercise after the cold.
Cricket on the grass, blasting
for runs—if I return from walking
the baby into a quiet area. Motion's
soothing and she must sleep.
The pitbull racing up to the stroller:
last month two infants mauled—one
to death. A furor—to put down
the killer dog or not. Descendants
of Europe revelling in underspeak
and dogshavemorerightsthanhumans—
a yogic concept returning: all souls
and life are equal, some more
Orwellian so: the letter which never
got published. Kill the sonofabitch
dog and charge the owner for criminal
negligence or manslaughter (who will
publish this poem?) or better, put
the sonofadog down too. So justice
is blind and must be swift! What's new?
Glare to glare. And the dog runs off—
hand on a pocketknife (your throat
or mine) and the small blue automatic
written into the Canada Geese story
blasting for respect in the northern
cold. Returning the waked up baby
—the what? The picnic grown
larger—those who will play cricket
and those who will not: gin, whisky
rum. One clump: how to invest your
money—*RRSP compared to real estate!*
It's wasting money to rent the loud—
mouth-rich holding court. Wealth does
what to what! Miami too hot; spent two
years, too slow, too much booze
and sun. I make more money here
and the house, my house's still here

—yuh see all those fleeing
the New York cold moving back…
In my, this group no politics, no
talk of money; only serious laughter
come join us, the large moustaches
the anti-intellectual, we make no
pretence to knowledge, *tek a drink—*
yuh know dhe story of the whiteman
who mispronounced Gopinauth's name
at work: go-pee-nat *ha ha* or the man
who masturbated on the jacket of a
musician in the dark concerthall—
because he was playing all night
like a cunt ha ha! The spousecall
look over heads; yes yes
I'm coming. It's getting dark
and the kids must go to bed.

TIMELESS MONEY, AGELESS MIND

Knocking Hindu India with words
like brittle bricks. This is scholarship
and I a novelist, see my prizes!
I'm published by The Canadian Publishers
you know. Was there a wrong turn
an ancestor's conversion, or somewhere
in Africa haunted out by the Amin
expulsion. A Goan unacknowledged
as subject for a novel. Tribe is tribe
and race race, Muslim Muslim!
An MD or PhD in physics—Chopra
reading Lewis' Arrowsmith at 16
or 18: I *will have you know an MD's*
an author. And why not? We hold your
lives in our hands—it's natural to
crossover to Merlin. But why can't I

99

heal too, good doctor? *Ayurvedically*
you do—words are more than wind
more than mantra more than scalpel
more than laser fixes. I've always
wanted to be a great healer
in the west i.e. rapping Hindu India!

THE UN-NAMED OF NORTHERN SEASONS

These are of those summers
which were too short.
So many places unvisited
—having fallen
for that annualholiday pride
among colleagues and friends
O so marvellous!—we are
not only well read
but well travelled
nowhere on floating fantasies
in the Atlantic or the Gulf
makebelieveland. But here
the cottage—O the cottage.

These are of those summers
which went too quickly
bodywatching on the sand
of some little lake
or in a mall escaping the heat
of workweek and when finally
in the park all those friends
the kids to look out for
those men—so far you thank
something equality lags behind
in pedophilia.

It is growing cool again
cold and the leaves colour
fall before you had a chance
to get past chlorophyll-lessness
anticipating first snowfall—
every cell crying out
what am I doing here what
am I doing here. You are
leaving. The baby has grown
too big for the swing
and you wake up one day
to white hair sticking out
your nose. And these moments
of dissatisfaction before
instead you see the cup half-full
for all those trees you loved
in the early summers, unclassified.
Named only in littleread books.

BOOK PACKAGE

Three collections arriving today
one package. This is the first day
of a summer we will remember
if nothing, for the heat—fifteen
hours of daylight. Another packet
telling of the driving time to Texas.
Who had said, another wouldbe
poet, the old man greenhousing
multiples of flowers before the fall:
nostalgia and memory—all those
For X. For Y. For C poems. Or
those After Z pieces, famous pattern.

You know when your poems are
empty. Even Walcott had those
For S, for Susan, for Sontag lapses.

Not this poet sending his threebook
package: rain falling sun lives
lived in characters and creators
colour not merely local—immortelles
poincianas, saman, sugarcane stalks
up in smoke like small black rotors
waiting to disintegrate on skin—
tomorrow the sweet canejuice, sugar—

the bitter rum of yesterday and now: If
these were mine, three books at a time! I'd
have nothing acerbic to say, nothing.

REALIGNING STARS

Toss a lemon ball
into sun and catch it
unaware love looks through
her window wistfully: *your
safe palms and fingers!*
In the rented garden
roses and red gladiolus
the clump of suckers

in a corner ripening
a bunch of bananas.
But when we go public
love must not... There
is that scent all over.

To head for night
and warm wroughtiron
chairs waiting
for rain. To reach up
and gather handfuls
of fluff, realign stars
of a sudden consternation.
But no washing is enough.

DHARMAKEEPING

And so if you don't see
me for awhile straddling
any pages of journals
or find any book forthcoming
or hear any poem performed
publicly in celebration
of the lives and times
of those aging older writers
my turn comes soon—don't
look for Theroux-Naipaul
tellalls, if you love you love.

And so if you don't see
me for awhile you'll know
to find me in grihastha
ashram, enjoying the all
of domesticity, blowing bubbles
for the kids (this is too
wordy—where the striking
imagery?) explaining what
I don't know—owning up
to unpreparedness: a lie
nobody's ever fully prepared
for parenthood? Even those men
waiting patiently with hooks
on the mouth of the river
are still worth a goodmorning.

But now we are playing cars—
imaginary money changing
hands at the imaginary gaspump
heading off on the windowsill
highway for Vancouver, Montreal
Mexico, and teaching places, Miami.

So if you see no poems
it is not that I've switched

to a fiction of sorts
or gaming with toys
I've never had and so
—newspaper shrinks!—
if you don't see
me for awhile, or ever again
mark it to love greater
than nirvana: this dharma
greater than love
no glossary can explain.

WINTER'S DINING HALL

(Searching for El Dorado:
Celebrating the Arrival of Indians in the West Indies)

There is the butterfly
and there the speaker
introducing the table:
doctor from Calgary
and Dr from New Delhi
Dr from York and last
Doctor from London—brilliant
scholar, leader, pioneer will
give the feature address—

the insect already over
a concrete rafter, teasing
a tendril of light, the day
trying to cling to a skylight
square window thirty or forty
—we still measure in feet—
above the planters' heads
the kurmis were a planter's class
of UP or Bihar. Do I sound
like Jagan: Politician demagogue

fire and passion and rhetoric?
Man wah mih guh tell yuh?
Abhi come from same country!

A time we were there, that
very podium. And HE returned
to hear the poetry; standing
on a balcony in the ceiling—
if you speak about vision
about thinking big, these early
ancestors had it—those Dutch
who would build five thousand
miles of canals, irrigate
a malaria infested jungle
cultivate that hostile tract
of South American land! A note
about the labour—those slaves
from Africa, don't forget, whose
sweat filled those canals still...

Or the Indian coolies—
extraordinary agriculturalists
those Kurmis who coaxed love
from that soil whose soul
possessed them. Destitute
in 19th century India
and all this land wasting!

The butterfly popping over
that rafter. Who cares. An air
vent somewhere providing release
from the bombast and summer heat
—you know the story of the Tiger
in the stars chasing the shipboard
voyage: three months across
the water from Calcutta to Demerara?

105

And if you think kala pani meant
black water! There's no black
water in all the oceans. So was kala
time as in Harris or Tagore?
That water which transposed us
across space and time and Africa
and Europe. That dhotied immigrant
who loved the night deck wasn't even
seeing tigers but stars—a cosmos
beyond reincarnation or El Dorado.

SIBBALD'S POINT: JULY 1

Almost to the month and day
ten years revolving or last year
waiting for the thunderstorms
—you can check this from
the weather office records
one cannot lie in poetry
distillate of language!—
this strip was wider—larger
the island smaller and nothing
would make us go into the murky
water—further out green green
as the eyes and endless beach
offering up endless feminine buns
turned up to sun or pudendums—
all smaller today or vision
larger kites dot the skyline
a raffle of red maple leaves
on paper nationalism
or gratitude from foreign lands
later south another border
to cross blank pages—a year
and that woman kneeling
in string bikini in the sand

106

teaching her infant—those
flocks of tiny fish swimming
through our legs are minnows
I didn't know until now
this lake possessed so many
lobsters dead or dying or stunned
washing up to the shore—and after
a year—or ten—The Book still
unfinished. It has been a long time
and we still didn't know this was
goodbye—a little affair all it takes
to wash away so many years.

AGAIN

or times when the little kiskidee
is all it takes to beat off
the invincible carrion hawk—
and chickens run unafraid
scratching dust in sunshine
searching the green grass
for flakes of life or the long
sweet kiss of a supplicant
love —eyes relighting bodies
reliving all that pleasure and pain
emanating from yourself infectious
sometimes it's just so long until
and yet you would rather not
hear that word again

NEXT TO GOD

You can crisscross the room
as many times as you want
look out across Montreal
at remnants of the Du Maurier
Jazz Festival theatre yesterday
the ebullience of Francophone
youths blaring horns and waving
tricolours at France's World Cup.

You can worry about your sleepy
unfed baby or the restless infant
—how many times race around
a glass cage in four hours?
Glare at the bridge across
the St Lawrence or the cross
above you on Mount Royal—it
doesn't matter what affidavit
you were not required to bring

I am asking for one now
which is entirely at my discretion—
lest you forget: next to god
is a US consular officer
granting—or not—immigrant visas!

A WRITER LIKE YOU

Riding tall in the saddle
of a Los Angeles hill
singing, speaking, living
only Sinatra even now not dead—
a house overlooking the pacific
two cars in the garage
a complete workshop to fix
anything; the do-it-yourselves

108

on handy shelves. *Fixers can*
take you to the cleaners—if
you didn't need a license
to practice home medicine!
I've put both kids through
college—man but the only thing
missing is the literary life—
not the starving artist thing
mind you. America's a barbaric
moneydriving society why come
here? Canada's so good to writers.
Man I tell yuh, if I had gone
there instead I woulda've been
a writer too—a writer like you!

THE TICK OF TOCK

Ticking of the tock
an elusive quietude
ripe like a mango
to be pricked—the sweet
juice squeezed out
or sucked—the edible skin
nibbled by a baby waking
the song of coo
a dove would understand
your spouse's relations
dropping their odysseys
at your door—a siren
wail; island of Circe
the winds the winds
let loose by untrusting
put your fingers in your
ears and pass the laughter
somewhere again some place
O when?—a waveless
ocean a windlessness
the tick of tock

109

LITERATURE'S WHOREDOM

And when one by one
they became writers of the revolution
like pujaris and certain Brahmin
priests; mere chanters of nonexistent
virtues of the comrade great leader
and had their works published
and their banner verses acclaimed
our lips hardened, closed
never we said never never never
dispersing to London New York
Toronto, cutting as agents suggest
as editors dictate—not agreeing but…
entering literature's whoredom

NOTES

"NO ELEGY FOR DR J": Dr Cheddi Bharat Jagan (1918-1997), charismatic, and dynamic Guyanese of Indian ancestry, was author of several books, including the classic *The West On Trial*. He studied in the US, where he met and married Janet Rosenberg, before returning alone to the colony of British Guiana in 1943. He was the founder of what became the People's Progressive Party, and in the first election under universal adult suffrage in the colony in 1953, his party swept the polls. However, after only 133 days in office, the British government suspended the constitution and sent in troops, claiming a "communist conspiracy." Dr Jagan's party again won the next elections in 1957 and 1962, and he became the first Premier of the colony. His government was destabilized (with documented American involvement) in the period following 1962—with fires, looting, and near civil war between the two main ethnic groups, people of African and of Indian ancestry. The British redrew the electoral boundaries so that even though his party won the largest block of votes, his party did not get a clear majority. The British granted independence to the colony under the leadership of LFS Burnham, a man of African ancestry. Burnham's regime was characterized by massively rigged elections, which have been well documented, violence, assassinations, corruption, and racism against the Indians, and it held on to power for almost 30 years, until the first free and fair elections since independence in 1992. At this election, monitored by an international team of observers, which included former US President Jimmy Carter, Dr Jagan became the first elected President of the Republic of Guyana. Dr Jagan died, in office, in 1997.

"DISMEMBERING H-INDIA": Patanjali's *Yoga Sutra*—one of the earliest and most authoritative treatise on Yoga; the Great Temple of Somnatha, considered one of seven wonders of the ancient world, was located in Gujarat. Several Muslim invaders destroyed this temple at different times.

"METHODIST HOSPITAL, BROOKLYN": *Bigan*—eggplant, a vegetable of Indian origin; *Dictatortime*—a reference to the regime of LFS Burnham, Prime Minister, and then self proclaimed Executive President of Guyana. Burnham ruled from 1966, to his death in office

111

in 1985, through a series of blatantly rigged elections. During Burnham's reign of terror, Guyanese, largely of Indian ancestry, fled by the thousands for England, Canada, and the United States. The undeclared racial policy of the regime sponsored and supported the blatant discrimination, repression, and physical intimidation of Indians in all walks of life. This is a pattern which continues today. NS—National Service. This was introduced by the Burnham regime, and it became compulsory to serve National Service in order to graduate from the University of Guyana. It was also a successful instrument to restrict and stop Indians—especially Indian women—from attending university. Up to that time, most of the graduates of the University of Guyana were Indians.

"DHARMAKEEPERS": *Pujaris*—priests who mainly perform Hindu rituals. *Pandits*—people who are learned, experts in philosophy and science, and masters in their area of expertise, who may also perform rituals. *Khajurao*—A series of temple structures in India, considered masterpieces of architecture and art, and famed world wide for their "erotic" carvings.

"DR WRITER": *Govapuri*—ancient Indian name of the present day Indian state of Goa.

"ANOTHER COOLIE POET": *Dunks, mango pineapple story*: This story, derogatory to people of African ancestry in this version, has many variations.

"BACKDAM POET": *Jadubance*—Magic man, spiritual healer. *Nishad*—A village chief, who has achieved eternal fame in the *Ramayana*.

"YATRA": *Krishna*—Hindu incarnation of God. *Praphupadha*—Founder of the Krishna Consciousness Movement in the West. *Chandan*—Sandalwood, a paste made with sandalwood, and used to make markings on the forehead of a devotee. *Jaganauth*—Another incarnation of god. *Harinam*—In the Name of Hari. Hari is another name of Krishna. *Dholak*—Indian hand drum.Sindhur—vermilion. Sindhur is associated with marriage, and in a Hindu wedding, the application of sindhur to the bride's forehead and head by the bridegroom signifies that they have entered into the sacred bond of matrimony. *Bansuri*—A bamboo flute. Krishna is often, in his role as divine musician, depicted with this bamboo flute.

"THE CANADIAN NATIONAL EXHIBITION": *Neem*—The Margosa plant. A plant of Indian origin which is sacred to Hindus. This is a plant of great medicinal value in India and was long used in Ayurvedic medicines. Recently a giant American multinational has patented the name *neem* and has been in the American court system trying to prevent Indian manufacturers from using the Indian word on their products. *Khanda*—From the Sanskrit, origin of the word "candy." *Raj Kapoor*—famous Indian actor film maker.

"THIS NORTHERN SKY": *Ahirs*—a caste of cattle herders. *Chateying*—licking. This is an anglicization of the Hindi verb *chatna*, "to lick." *Vasudeva*—the father of Krishna.

"BLACK MONDAY: GEORGETOWN, JANUARY 12, 1998—FROM AFAR": On this day, in the continuing racial tension in Guyana, Blacks were incited to violence, and randomly attacked and raped scores of Indians in Georgetown. A call from Indian groups for a government inquiry has been ignored. *Labaria*—A deadly snake. *Cuffy Monster*—A monument in black stone, in the shape of a man of African ancestry, declared the "National Monument" by the Burnham regime, in a country where, at the time, Indians made up 51% of the population, and Blacks less than 40%. *Jhalls*—Brass cymbals. *Chakras*—In the Mahabharata, Krishna's circular weapon, which scholars believe to be a nuclear missile of some sort.

"DENNIS STREET": This is the street in an outlying suburb of Georgetown, where the city headquarters of American Cult Leader Jim Jones and his People's Temple were located. The most gruesome of the 900 odd murder/suicides occurred here. An ex-US- marine, reportedly on the orders of Jim Jones, slit the throats of the occupants of this house, which included children. The blood from the murders remained in the bathroom of the deserted house for years after.

I grew up on this street, and have had some of the most wonderful, and painful, experiences of my life, here.

ACKNOWLEDGMENTS

are due to

the following publications: *Ariel, Indo Caribbean Review, India World* and *Wasafiri*—in which several of these poems appeared.

THE CANADA COUNCIL for a grant, which facilitated the completion of this book.